Collins

The Shan Maths Project

For the English National Curriculum

Series Editor: Professor Lianghuo Fan
UK Curriculum Consultant: Paul Broadbent

Practice Book  3

William Collins' dream of knowledge for all began with the publication of his first book in 1819. A self-educated mill worker, he not only enriched millions of lives, but also founded a flourishing publishing house. Today, staying true to this spirit, Collins books are packed with inspiration, innovation and practical expertise. They place you at the centre of a world of possibility and give you exactly what you need to explore it.

Collins. Freedom to teach.

Published by Collins
An imprint of HarperCollins*Publishers* Ltd.
The News Building
1 London Bridge Street
London SE 1 9GF

Browse the complete Collins catalogue at
www. collins. co. uk

© HarperCollins*Publishers* Limited 2016
© Professor Lianghuo Fan 2016
© East China Normal University Press Ltd. 2016

10 9 8 7 6 5 4 3 2

ISBN: 978-0-00-814464-7

The Shanghai Maths Project (for the English National Curriculum) is a collaborative effort between HarperCollins, East China Normal University Press Ltd. and Professor Lianghuo Fan and his team. Based on the latest edition of the award-wining series of learning resource books, *One Lesson One Exercise*, by East China Normal University Press Ltd. in Chinese, the series of Practice Books is published by HarperCollins after adaptation following the English National Curriculum.

Practice book Year 3 is translated and developed by Professor Lianghuo Fan with assistance of Ellen Chen, Ming Ni, Huiping Xu and Dr. Lionel Pereira-Mendoza, with Paul Broadbent as UK curriculum consultant.

British Library Cataloguing in Publication Data
A Catalogue record for this publication is available from the British Library.

Series Editor: Professor Lianghuo Fan
UK Curriculum Consultant: Paul Broadbent
Commissioned by Lee Newman
Project Managed by Fiona McGlade and Mike Appleton
Design by Kevin Robbins and East China Normal University Press Ltd.
Typesetting by East China Normal University Press Ltd.
Cover illustration by Daniela Geremia
Production by Rachel Weaver
Printed by Grafica Veneta S. p. A

Contents

Contents

Chapter 10   Let's practise geometry

Answers / 207

Chapter 1   Revising and improving

1.1   Revision for addition and subtraction of two-digit numbers

Learning objective

Add and subtract two-digit numbers

Basic questions

1. Work these out mentally. Write the answers.

    $63 + 9 =$ $75 + 24 =$ $84 - 16 =$ $70 - 35 =$

    $34 + 16 =$ $48 + 25 =$ $63 - 36 =$ $93 - 53 =$

    $38 + 25 =$ $27 + 44 =$ $74 - 58 =$ $60 - 42 =$

    $36 + 18 =$ $67 - 27 =$ $50 - 43 =$ $90 + 10 =$

2. Add three numbers.

    $21 + 23 + 50 =$ $36 + 44 + 13 =$ $13 + 30 + 37 =$

    $23 + 20 + 40 =$ $67 + 25 + 12 =$ $42 + 26 + 24 =$

    $60 + 18 + 11 =$ $21 + 44 + 12 =$ $35 + 16 + 40 =$

3. Subtract three numbers.

    $72 - 33 - 12 =$ $54 - 27 - 18 =$ $67 - 21 - 22 =$

    $68 - 45 - 18 =$ $65 - 56 - 3 =$ $86 - 35 - 24 =$

    $88 - 12 - 51 =$ $79 - 19 - 26 =$ $77 - 56 - 6 =$

4. Complete these mixed addition and subtraction calculations.

    $87 + 10 - 27 =$ $57 + 31 - 27 =$ $54 - 52 + 17 =$

    $96 - 63 + 41 =$ $74 - 47 + 15 =$ $88 - 46 + 55 =$

    $54 - 33 + 21 =$ $36 - 18 + 9 =$ $77 + 18 - 34 =$

5 Fill in the brackets.

(　　) + 41 = 56　　　82 − (　　) = 55　　　(　　) − 36 = 39

36 + (　　) = 71　　　80 − (　　) = 29　　　34 = (　　) − 34

6 Application problems.

　　£18　　　　　　　£15　　　　　　　£46　　　　　　　£25

(a) John bought a and a . How much did they cost

him in total?

(b) John paid for a watch with a 50 pound note. How much change

did he get?

(c) John bought a basketball and a watch. How much cheaper is the

basketball than the watch?

Challenge and extension question

7 Insert + or − between the numbers to make each equation true.

(a) 1　2　3　5　4 = 1

(b) 1　2　3　4　5　6 = 1

2

1.2 Addition and subtraction (1)

 Learning objective

Add and subtract two-digit numbers

 Basic questions

1 Work these out mentally. Write the answers.

$35 + 8 =$ $63 - 8 =$ $53 - 6 =$ $(\quad) - 35 = 20$

$54 + 5 =$ $35 + 65 =$ $74 - 60 - 3 =$ $(\quad) + 81 = 81$

$91 - 9 =$ $42 + 9 =$ $40 + 50 - 5 =$ $(\quad) - 7 + 5 = 44$

2 Use the column method to calculate.

$36 + 48 =$ $82 - 25 =$ $70 - 32 + 49 =$

3 Write each number sentence and calculate.

(a)   27 apples   18 pears
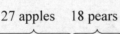
How many fruits are there in total?

Number sentence: _____

(b) There are 27 apples. How many pears are there?

There are 45 fruits in total.

Number sentence: _____

(c)   25 boys

There are 6 more girls than boys.

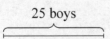

How many girls are there?

Number sentence: _____

(d)   38 boys

How many more boys are there than girls?

29 girls

Number sentence: _____

4 Write each number sentence and calculate.

(a) Grandma bought 56 eggs. After using some eggs, she had 19 left. How many eggs did grandma use?

Number sentence: _____

Answer: _____

(b)

Number sentence: _____

Answer: _____

 Challenge and extension question

5 Write each number sentence and calculate.

£47   £24   £38   £76

(a) How much cheaper is the toy aeroplane than the toy car?

Number sentence: _____

(b) If you have £100, how many toys can you buy? Will you get some change? If so, how much is the change?

1.3　Addition and subtraction (2)

Learning objective

Add and subtract two-digit numbers

Basic questions

1 Work these out mentally. Write the answers.

$47 - 25 =$	$18 + 49 =$	$82 - 16 =$	$51 - 7 =$
$76 + 18 =$	$9 + 81 =$	$38 - 20 =$	$77 - 14 =$
$32 + 49 =$	$15 + 47 =$	$65 - 19 =$	$36 - 18 =$

2 Fill in the brackets.

$34 + 47 = ($　$)$　　　$93 - 29 = ($　$)$　　　$($　$) - 25 = 39$

$($　$) + 47 = 71$　　　$93 - ($　$) = 74$　　　$($　$) - 35 = 39$

$($　$) + 47 = 61$　　　$93 - ($　$) = 54$　　　$($　$) - 45 = 39$

$34 + ($　$) = 51$　　　$93 - ($　$) = 34$　　　$80 - ($　$) = 39$

3 Write each number sentence and calculate.

(a)

15 flew away.　10 remain.

How many were there at first?

Number sentence：＿＿＿＿＿＿

(b)

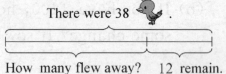

There were 38 .

How many flew away?　12 remain.

Number sentence：＿＿＿＿＿＿

(c)

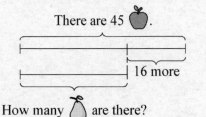

There are 45 .

16 more

How many are there?

Number sentence：＿＿＿＿＿＿

(d)

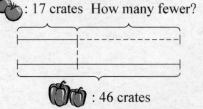

: 17 crates　How many fewer?

: 46 crates

Number sentence：＿＿＿＿＿＿

4 Answer these application problems.

£24   £32   £68   £48

(a) Tom bought 2 toys for exactly £100. Which toys did he buy?

Number sentence: _____

(b) Oliver bought a toy helicopter and a skateboard. How much did he spend?

Number sentence: _____

(c) Anya had £54 and bought a toy telephone. How much did she have left?

Number sentence: _____

    Challenge and extension question

5 Replace the letters with non-zero numbers to make each calculation true.

(a)
$$\begin{array}{cc} M & M \\ + & M \\ \hline 8 & 4 \end{array}$$

M=(   )

(b)
$$\begin{array}{cc} A & M \\ - M & A \\ \hline 7 & 2 \end{array}$$

A=(   ) M=(   )

1.4　Calculating smartly

Learning objective

Use strategies to add and subtract two-digit numbers

Basic questions

1 Fill in the brackets.

$38 + ($ 　 $) = 40$ 　　 $60 + ($ 　 $) = 70$ 　　 $($ 　 $) + 54 = 60$

$($ 　 $) + 71 = 80$ 　　 $45 + ($ 　 $) = 50$ 　　 $26 + ($ 　 $) = 30$

2 Fill in the boxes.

(a) $48 + 17 = \Box$
$\downarrow$
$49 + 16$
$\downarrow$
$50 + 15 = \Box$

(b) $55 + 27 = \Box$
$\downarrow$
$54 + 28$
$\downarrow$
$53 + 29$
$\downarrow$
$52 + 30 = \Box$

(c) $72 - 33 = \Box$
$\downarrow$
$71 - 32$
$\downarrow$
$70 - 31$
$\downarrow$
$69 - 30 = \Box$

(d) $64 - 17 = \Box$
$\downarrow$
$65 - 18$
$\downarrow$
$66 - 19$
$\downarrow$
$67 - 20 = \Box$

(e) $49 \; + \; 16 \; = \Box$
　$\downarrow +1$ 　$\downarrow -1$
　$50 \; + \; 15 \; = \Box$

(f) $75 \; - \; 36 \; = \Box$
　$\downarrow +4$ 　$\downarrow +4$
　$79 \; - \; 40 \; = \Box$

(g) $38 \; + \; 45 \; = \Box$
　$\downarrow \Box$ 　$\downarrow \Box$
　$\Box \; + \; \Box \; = \Box$

(h) $63 \; - \; 39 \; = \Box$
　$\downarrow \Box$ 　$\downarrow \Box$
　$\Box \; - \; \Box \; = \Box$

3 Fill in the boxes to complete each calculation.

(a) $38 + 14 = 40 + \boxed{} = \boxed{}$ (b) $56 - 27 = \boxed{} - 30 = \boxed{}$

(c) $17 + 49 = \boxed{} + \boxed{} = \boxed{}$ (d) $93 - 47 = \boxed{} - \boxed{} = \boxed{}$

(e) $\boxed{} + 28 = 44 + \boxed{} = 74$ (f) $73 - \boxed{} = \boxed{} - 30 = \boxed{}$

(g) $24 + 69 = \boxed{} + \boxed{} = \boxed{} + \boxed{} = \boxed{} + \boxed{} = \boxed{} + \boxed{}$

(h) $72 - 34 = \boxed{} - \boxed{} = \boxed{} - \boxed{} = \boxed{} - \boxed{} = \boxed{} - \boxed{}$

4 Draw lines to match the calculations that have the same answer.

$55 + 28$	$60 - 13$
$13 + 48$	$53 + 30$
$62 - 15$	$78 - 40$
$74 - 36$	$10 + 51$

Challenge and extension question

5 Xin was adding two numbers. He mistook the number 7 in the ones place of one of the addends for 5, the number 4 in its tens place for 6, and so got an answer of 92 as a result. The correct answer should be (   ).

1.5 What number should be in the box?

Learning objective

Solve missing number addition and subtraction problems

Basic questions

1 Fill in the boxes.

$52 + \boxed{} = 81$ $47 - \boxed{} = 9$ $\boxed{} - 25 = 39$

$81 - 52 = \boxed{}$ $47 - 9 = \boxed{}$ $39 + 25 = \boxed{}$

$33 + \boxed{} = 67$ $56 - \boxed{} = 28$ $\boxed{} - 24 = 44$

$\boxed{} + 18 = 18$ $\boxed{} - 37 = 63$ $67 - \boxed{} = 28$

$64 - \boxed{} = 34$ $\boxed{} - 73 = 19$ $48 + \boxed{} = 82$

2 Look at the diagrams and fill in the boxes.

(a)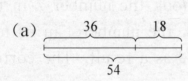

$\boxed{} + \boxed{} = \boxed{}$ $\boxed{} + \boxed{} = \boxed{}$

$\boxed{} - \boxed{} = \boxed{}$ $\boxed{} - \boxed{} = \boxed{}$

(b)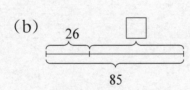

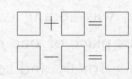

$26 + \boxed{} = 85$

$85 - 26 = \boxed{}$

(c)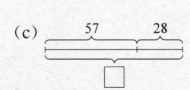

$\boxed{} - 57 = 28$

$57 + 28 = \boxed{}$

(d)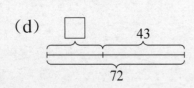

$\boxed{} + 43 = 72$ $72 - \boxed{} = 43$

$72 - 43 = \boxed{}$ $72 - 43 = \boxed{}$

3 Write each number sentence and calculate.

(a)   There were 72 🐟 in the pond at first.

34 🐟 were left.   How many 🐟 swam away?

Number sentence：_____

(b)

There are 15 🧒   There are 36 🪁

How many children are there altogether?

Number sentence：_____

(c) There were 12 🐦 in a tree.   How many more 🐦 joined them?

There are now 21 birds.

Number sentence：_____

Challenge and extension question

4 Write > or < in each box based on the number sentence given.

$\blacksquare + 17 = 26 + \bullet$ $\blacksquare - 9 = \bullet - 15$ $\blacksquare + 8 = \bullet - 8$

$\blacksquare \square \bullet$ $\blacksquare \square \bullet$ $\blacksquare \square \bullet$

1.6 Let's revise multiplication

 Learning objective

Use the relationship between 2, 4 and 8 times tables

 Basic questions

1 Write the multiplication facts.

(a) Fill in the multiplication table.

(b) Circle the multiplication facts that can be used to write only one multiplication sentence and one division sentence.

(c) Using the same coloured pen, colour the multiplication facts with the same products.

(d) Use the multiplication table to tell the relationship between multiplications of 2, 4 and 8.

(e) Can you get any other results by looking at the multiplication table?

1×1=1									
1×2=2	2×2=4								
	2×3=6								
		3×4=12	4×4=16						
				5×5=25					
1×8=8							8×8=64		
1×9=9									
								9×10=90	10×10=100

2 Draw lines to help each cat find the right house.

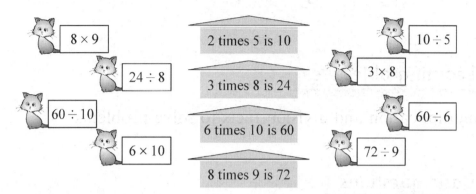

8 × 9

24 ÷ 8

60 ÷ 10

6 × 10

2 times 5 is 10

3 times 8 is 24

6 times 10 is 60

8 times 9 is 72

10 ÷ 5

3 × 8

60 ÷ 6

72 ÷ 9

3 Fill in the brackets.

Use the multiplication facts to fill in: 20	The quotient is 3
( )×( )=20 ( )×( )=20	( )÷( )=3 ( )÷( )=3
( )×( )=20 ( )×( )=20	( )÷( )=3 ( )÷( )=3

Use the multiplication facts to fill in: 24	The quotient is 5
( )×( )=24 ( )×( )=24	( )÷( )=5 ( )÷( )=5
( )×( )=24 ( )×( )=24	( )÷( )=5 ( )÷( )=5

Use the multiplication facts to fill in: 30	The quotient is 8
( )×( )=30 ( )×( )=30	( )÷( )=8 ( )÷( )=8
( )×( )=30 ( )×( )=30	( )÷( )=8 ( )÷( )=8

 ## Challenge and extension question

4 Write the missing numbers.

( )×5 = ( )×10

( )×2 = ( )×4 = ( )×8

( )×3 = ( )×6 = ( )×9

1.7　Games of multiplication and division

 Learning objective

Use multiplication and division facts to solve problems

Basic questions

1. Look at the diagrams and fill in the brackets. Then write the number sentences.

(a) ☆☆☆
◇◇◇◇◇◇◇◇◇

There are (　　) times as many (　　) as (　　).
Number sentence：_____

(b)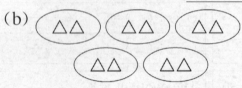

There are (　　) groups of (　　) in (　　).
Number sentence：_____

(c) How many footballs are there in total? Group the footballs in two different ways and write the number sentences.

Number sentence：   Number sentence：
(　　)×(　　)+(　　)=(　　)　(　　)×(　　)+(　　)=(　　)
Number sentence：   Number sentence：
(　　)×(　　)−(　　)=(　　)　(　　)×(　　)−(　　)=(　　)

2 Write each number sentence and calculate.

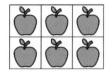 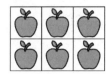  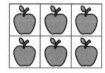

(a) How many days will the apples last if 6 are eaten each day?

Number sentence: _____

(b) How many days will the apples last if 3 are eaten each day?

Number sentence: _____

(c) How many days will the apples last if 7 are eaten each day? How many apples will be left over on the last day?

Number sentence: _____

3 Draw the number of shapes as indicated and then fill in the brackets and the number sentences below.

In the first row, draw 2 ☆ _____

In the second row, draw 4 △ _____

In the third row, there are 4 times as many ◯ as ☆ in the first row:  _____

(a) There are (   ) times as many ◯ as △.

☐◯☐=☐

(b) 5 times the number of ◯ is (   ).

☐◯☐=☐

 Challenge and extension question

4 All the children in a class are assembled in the sports field. They form exactly 5 rows of the same number of children. Tom is in the second row. He is in the fourth place from the left. He is also in the fourth place from the right. How many children are there in the class?

Unit test 1

1 Work these out mentally. Write the answers.

$46 + 19 =$	$54 - 45 =$	$1 \times 10 =$	$10 \div 5 =$
$32 - 7 =$	$67 + 30 =$	$4 \times 12 =$	$36 \div 9 =$
$63 - 42 =$	$72 + 17 =$	$5 \times 8 =$	$35 \div 5 =$

2 Complete the mixed addition and subtraction calculations.

$51 - 42 + 53 =$	$77 - 65 - 6 =$	$71 - 52 + 36 =$
$75 + 24 - 23 =$	$32 + 45 - 38 =$	$81 - 45 + 36 =$
$63 + 12 - 42 =$	$53 - 37 + 15 =$	$63 - 23 + 28 =$

3 Fill in the brackets.

$53 + (\quad) = 70$	$(\quad) + 76 = 98$	$(\quad) - 72 = 7$
$49 = 18 + (\quad)$	$5 = (\quad) - 35$	$(\quad) + 18 = 18$
$5 \times (\quad) = 50$	$8 \times 12 = (\quad)$	$32 \div (\quad) = 8$
$(\quad) \div 2 = 7$	$(\quad) \times 10 = 4 \times 5$	$36 \div 4 = (\quad) \div 2$

4 Write each number sentence and calculate.

(a) ○○○ ······ ○○

⎵⎵⎵⎵⎵⎵⎵⎵
65○

There are 28 △ fewer than ○.

How many △ are there?

Number sentence: _____

Answer: There are (   ) △.

(b) 16 pears were eaten.   How many were left?

There were 30 pears altogether.

Number sentence: _____

Answer: There were (   ) pears left.

(c)

24 candies were eaten. 38 candies were left.

How many candies were there at first?

Number sentence: _____

Answer: There were (   ) candies at first.

(d)

? copies

Storybook

45 copies 16 copies

Science book

Number sentence: _____

Answer: There are (   ) storybooks.

(e)

37 bundles

Rose   How many more?

Lily

72 bundles

Number sentence: _____

Answer: There are (   ) more bundles of lilies than roses.

(f) A bus can seat 40 people. A car can seat 4 people. How many times as many people can a bus seat as a car?

Number sentence: _____

Answer: A bus can seat (   ) times as many people as a car.

(g) A 72-metre long rope was cut into 9 equal pieces. How long is each piece?

Number sentence: _____

Answer: Each piece is (   ) long.

5 Write a suitable number in each bracket.

$$\begin{array}{r} 3\ (\ ) \\ +\ (\ )\ 6 \\ \hline 7\quad 7 \end{array}$$

$$\begin{array}{r} 8\ (\ ) \\ -\ (\ )\ 5 \\ \hline 4\quad 0 \end{array}$$

$$\begin{array}{r} (\ )\ 4 \\ +\ 3\ (\ ) \\ \hline 6\quad 3 \end{array}$$

$$\begin{array}{r} (\ )\ 6 \\ -\ 1\ (\ ) \\ \hline 4\quad 9 \end{array}$$

2.1   Multiplying and dividing by 7

 Learning objective

Multiply and divide by 7

 Basic questions

1 Fill in the brackets.

Two times seven is (　　　　).　Four times seven is (　　　　).

Seven times eight is (　　　　).　One times seven is (　　　　).

Seven times (　　　　) is forty-nine.

(　　　　) times seven is twenty-one.

(　　　　) times (　　　　) is sixty-three.

Ten times (　　　　) is seventy.

Eleven times seven is (　　　　).

(　　　　) times seven is eighty-four.

2 Draw lines to help each cat catch the right fish.

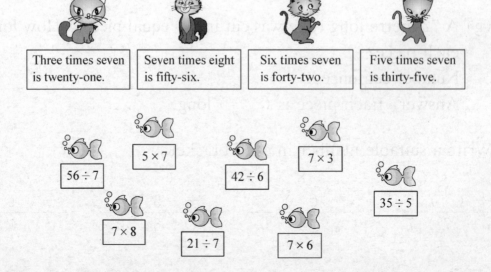

3 Calculate.

$1 \times 7 =$	$7 \times 4 =$	$35 \div 7 =$	$63 \div 9 =$
$0 \div 7 =$	$9 \times 7 =$	$14 \div 7 =$	$56 \div 7 =$
$7 \times 11 =$	$12 \times 7 =$	$84 \div 7 =$	$70 \div 7 =$

$49 = \boxed{} \times 7$ $\quad 3 = \boxed{} \div 7$ $\quad 77 = \boxed{} \times 7$ $\quad 10 = \boxed{} \div 7$

4 Application problems.

(a) 14 sweets were shared equally by 7 children. How many sweets did each child get?

Answer: _____

(b) In one week, Zoe used 3 pieces of paper every day. How many pieces of paper did she use in the whole week?

Answer: _____

(c) In Maths lessons for Class A, the teacher divides the children into 7 groups. There are 5 children in each group. How many children are there?

Answer: _____

Class B has 6 more children than Class A. How many children are there in Class B?

Answer: _____

Challenge and extension question

5 Use the numbers below to make number sentences. Who can make the most number sentences? (Hint: operations can be used on both sides of the equation.)

14, 42, 6, 7, 2, 4, 28, 35, 5

2.2 Multiplying and dividing by 3

 Learning objective

Multiply and divide by 3

 Basic questions

1 Complete the multiplication facts. Then write multiplication and division sentences.

Three times five　（　　　）times（　　　　）Three times（　　）
is（　　　　）.　　is thirty-three.　　　is eighteen.

_____　_____　_____

_____　_____　_____

_____　_____　_____

_____　_____　_____

2 Calculate.

$6 \times 3 =$　　　　$3 \times 8 =$　　　　$3 \times 9 =$　　　　$11 \times 3 =$

$7 \times 3 =$　　　　$3 \times 12 =$　　　　$30 \div 3 =$　　　　$5 \times 3 =$

$36 \div 3 =$　　　$2 \times 9 = (\quad) \times 3$　　$27 \div 9 = 3 \times (\quad)$

$4 \times (\quad) = 2 \times 6$　　$3 \times (\quad) = 12$　　$(\quad) \times 3 = 12 + 3$

3 Fill in the table.

Dividend	3		18	27		30	0
Divisor		7	6		3		3
Quotient	1	3		9	12	3	

4 Write each number sentence and calculate.

(a) What is the product of two threes?

Number sentence：_____

19

(b) How many threes should be subtracted from 15 so the result is 0?

Number sentence:_____

(c) What is 7 times 3?

Number sentence:_____

⑤ Application problems.

(a) Joe and his parents visited a museum. The admission ticket was £8 per person. How much did they have to pay?

Answer:_____

Joe paid with a £50 note. How much change should he get?

Answer:_____

(b) 6 ducks are on a river. There are 4 times as many ducks on the bank as on the river. How many ducks are on the bank?

Answer:_____

How many ducks are there altogether?

Answer:_____

Challenge and extension questions

6 A bag of sweets can be divided equally into 3 groups. It can also be divided equally into 6 groups. What could be the least number of sweets in the bag?

Answer:_____

❼ A monkey picked 24 peaches. She gave all the peaches to her two baby monkeys. The elder baby monkey got 2 times as many peaches as the younger one. How many peaches did the younger baby monkey get?

Answer:_____

How many peaches did the elder monkey get?

Answer:_____

2.3 Multiplying and dividing by 6

 Learning objective

Multiply and divide by 6

 Basic questions

① Write two multiplication sentences in numbers and the multiplication fact in words for each picture.

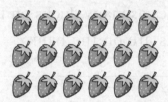

_____

_____

Multiplication fact：

_____

_____

Multiplication fact：

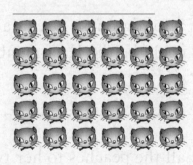

_____

_____

Multiplication fact：

_____

_____

Multiplication fact：

② Fill in the ◯ with >, < or =.

3×6 ◯ 9×2 6×12 ◯ 70 6×9 ◯ $5 \times 9 + 9$ $60 \div 10$ ◯ $66 \div 6$

③ Fill in the brackets.

12 = (   ) × (   ) = (   ) × (   ) = (   ) × (   )
36 = (   ) × (   ) = (   ) × (   ) = (   ) × (   )
18 = (   ) × (   ) = (   ) × (   ) = (   ) × (   )

④ Calculate.

6 × 5 =	7 × 6 =	9 × 6 =	24 ÷ 6 =
3 × 7 =	8 × 9 =	0 × 6 =	36 ÷ 4 =
3 × 11 =	6 × 11 =	12 × 6 =	66 ÷ 11 =
6 × 10 =	72 ÷ 6 =	6 = ( ) ÷ 6	11 = ( ) ÷ 6

⑤ Read the pictures and answer the questions below.

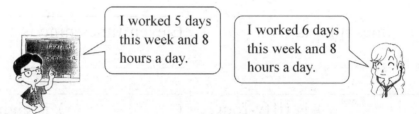

I worked 5 days this week and 8 hours a day.

I worked 6 days this week and 8 hours a day.

How many hours did Mum work in the week?
Answer: _____
How many fewer hours did Dad work than Mum in the week?
Answer: _____

 Challenge and extension questions

⑥ Given ○ + ○ + ○ + ○ = △ + □ , □ = △ + △ ,
if ○ = 6 , then △ = (   ).

⑦ Simon reads 6 pages of a book every day. He has read the book for 4 days. On the fifth day, Simon should start to read from page (   ).

2.4 Multiplying and dividing by 9

 Learning objective

Multiply and divide by 9

Basic questions

1 Recall the multiplication facts and write the answers.

One times nine is (   ).   Three times nine is (   ).

$1 \times 9 =$ _____   _____

$9 \times 1 =$ _____   _____

Four times nine is (   ).   Eleven times nine is (   ).

_____   _____

_____   _____

(   ) is fifty-four.   (   ) is eighteen.

_____   _____

_____   _____

2 Find the greatest number that will fill in each bracket.

$2 \times ($ $) < 19$ $10 \times ($ $) < 25$ $($ $) \times 9 < 23$

$5 \times ($ $) < 24$ $($ $) \times 5 < 54$ $($ $) \times 6 < 36$

$8 \times ($ $) < 20$ $($ $) \times 9 < 55$ $($ $) \times 9 < 100$

3 Choose three numbers from each group to write two multiplication sentences and two division sentences.

3, 9, 21, 7	6, 45, 5, 9	90, 9, 20, 10

_____   _____   _____

_____   _____   _____

_____   _____   _____

4 Application problems.

(a) A rabbit collected 54 carrots and gave all of them equally to 6 baby rabbits. How many carrots did each baby rabbit get?

Answer: _____

(b) Tom, Max and Emily went to Anya's home to celebrate her birthday. Anya's mother prepared food including chocolate, cake and fruit.

The four children shared 36 chocolate bars equally. How many bars did each child get?

Answer: _____

There were 9 bananas in a bunch. There were 3 bunches. How many bananas were there altogether?

Answer: _____

There were 9 pieces of cake in each box. How many boxes were there for 18 pieces of cake?

Answer: _____

Challenge and extension questions

5 Complete the number patterns.

9, 5, 18, 10, 27, 15, (   ), (   ).

1, 3, 7, 15, 31, (   ), (   ).

6 It took James 18 seconds to run from the first floor to the third floor. How many seconds did it take James to run from one floor to the next floor on average?

Answer: _____

How many seconds would it take James to run from the first floor to the eighth floor if he could keep the same speed?

Answer: _____

2.5 Relationships between multiplications of 3, 6 and 9

 Learning objective

Use the relationship between the 3, 6 and 9 times tables

 Basic questions

1. Group the objects and write the multiplication sentences for each picture.

3 in a group

(   ) × (   ) = (   )

(   ) × (   ) = (   )

6 in a group

(   ) × (   ) = (   )

(   ) × (   ) = (   )

9 in a group

(   ) × (   ) = (   )

(   ) × (   ) = (   )

2. Fill in the brackets.

$18 = 3 \times ($ $) = 6 \times ($ $) = 9 \times ($ $)$

$36 = ($ $) \times 4 = ($ $) \times 6 = 3 \times ($ $)$

$54 = ($ $) \times 9 = ($ $) \times 6 = ($ $) \times 3$

3 Write number sentences and then calculate.

(a) What is the sum of adding seven sixes together?

Number sentence: _____

(b) How many fours are there in 36?

Number sentence: _____

(c) How many threes should be subtracted from 24 so the result is 0? How many sixes?

Number sentence: _____

Number sentence: _____

4 Application problems.

(a) There are 9 roses. There are twice as many tulips as roses. How many tulips are there?

Answer: _____

If a bouquet of flowers is made up of 9 flowers, how many bouquets can be made up with these tulips and roses?

Answer: _____

(b) There are 6 bunches of balloons and there are 6 balloons in each bunch. The balloons are to be shared equally among 3 children. How many balloons will each child get?

Answer: _____

Challenge and extension questions

5 There is a bag of marbles. They can be counted in both threes and sixes without any left over. What could be the least number of marbles in the bag?

Answer: _____

6 A dog is 3 times as heavy as a cat. The cat is 6 times as heavy as a squirrel. The squirrel is twice as heavy as a chick. How many times as heavy is the dog as the chick?

Answer: _____

2.6 Multiplication table

Learning objective

Explore numbers in a multiplication table

Basic questions

1 Complete the multiplication table.

1 × 1 = 1									
	2 × 2 = 4								
		3 × 4 = 12							
			4 × 5 =						
						7 × 7 =			
				5 × 8 = 40					
								9 × 9 =	
									10 × 10 = 100

2 Fill in the brackets. Then write two multiplication sentences and two division sentences.

Four times seven is	Five times eight is	Six times eleven is
( ).	( ).	( ).

_____   _____   _____

_____   _____   _____

_____   _____   _____

_____   _____   _____

Three times (   ) is twelve.   Four times (   ) is twenty-four.   (   ) times nine is thirty-six.

_____   _____   _____

_____   _____   _____

_____   _____   _____

3 Look at the pictures and write the number sentences.

(a) ☆☆☆☆☆☆ ☆☆☆☆☆☆   □÷□=□   Multiplication fact：_____

Meaning：Dividing (   ) into (   ) equal groups, each group has (   ).

(b) ♡♡♡♡♡♡♡♡♡♡♡♡♡♡   □÷□=□   Multiplication fact：_____

Meaning：There are (   ) groups of (   ) in (   ).

(c) △△△△△△△△ △△△△△△△△ △△△△△△△△   □÷□=□   Multiplication fact：_____

Meaning：(   ) is (   ) times (   ).

(d) 9   □×□=□   Multiplication fact：_____

Meaning：(   ) times (   ) is (   ).

Challenge and extension question

4 Fill in each ◯ with a suitable operation symbol so that the equation is correct.

2 ◯ 2 ◯ 2 ◯ 2=0   2 ◯ 2 ◯ 2 ◯ 2=1

2 ◯ 2 ◯ 2 ◯ 2=2   2 ◯ 2 ◯ 2 ◯ 2=3

2.7 Posing multiplication and division questions (1)

 Learning objective

Write multiplication and division number sentences

 Basic questions

1 Look at each picture. Pose a question and then write a number sentence. The first one has been done for you.

(a)

Question: How many sweets are there in total?

Number sentence: $5 \times 4 = 20$ (sweets)

(b)

Question: _____

Number sentence: _____

(c)

Question: _____

Number sentence: _____

(d)

Question: _____

Number sentence: _____

29

2 Complete each sentence by choosing the correct phrase below. Then write each number sentence and find the answer.

A school held a sports day. Year 3 children took part in various activities.

25 children took part in the rope skipping.	16 children took part in a relay race.	42 children played football.

How many children played table tennis?	How many times as many children played football as table tennis?

(a) _____ and there were 4 running tracks. How many children ran on each running track?

Number sentence: _____

(b) _____ and each class sent 5 children to take part in the rope skipping. How many classes were there in Year 3?

Number sentence: _____

(c) _____ , which was 7 times as many as those paying table tennis. _____

Number sentence: _____

Challenge and extension questions

3 In a long distance race, Alvin was 60 metres ahead of Peter. Simon was 100 metres behind Alex. Peter was 20 metres behind Simon. Who was the first runner in the race?

Answer: _____

How many metres is the difference between the first runner and the last runner?

Answer: _____

4 Olivia's mum bought 16 apples. She gave half of the apples to Olivia's grandma. Then she gave half of the rest to Olivia. How many apples did Olivia's mum still have?

Answer: _____

2.8 Posing multiplication and division questions (2)

Learning objective

Write multiplication and division number sentences

Basic questions

① Read the paragraph below. Then choose suitable conditions and write questions that can be solved using multiplication and division. The first one has been done for you.

There are many flowers in a garden. There are 10 pots of roses with each pot containing 4 roses. There are 36 lilies. There are 9 pots of tulips with each pot containing 2 tulips, and there are 72 orchids planted in 9 pots. There are also 6 empty pots.

(a) Condition(s): There are 10 pots of roses with each pot containing 4 roses.

Question: How many roses are there in total?

Number sentence: $10 \times 4 = 40$

(b) Condition(s): _____

Question: _____

Number sentence: _____

(c) Condition(s): _____

Question: _____

Number sentence: _____

2 Application problems.

(a) James has made 10 origami cranes. Tom, Joan and Mary have each made as many origami cranes as James. How many origami cranes have they made altogether?

Answer: _____

(b) 9 metres was cut from a ribbon. It is now 5 times as long as the piece that was cut off. How long is the remaining piece?

Answer: _____

How long was the original ribbon?

Answer: _____

(c) Mary and her parents visited the zoo over the weekend. The ticket price was £10 per person. How much did they pay?

Answer: _____

(d) There were 6 birds in each tree. How many birds were there in 5 trees?

Answer: _____

After 18 birds flew away, how many birds were left?

Answer: _____

Challenge and extension questions

3 It took Simon 60 seconds to walk from the first floor to the third floor. How long would it take him to walk from the first floor to the sixth floor at the same speed?

Answer: _____

4 Fold a 16-metre rope in half. Then fold the rope again to obtain four pieces. How long is each piece?

Answer: _____

2.9 Using multiplication and addition to express a number

 Learning objective

Solve problems involving multiplication and addition

 Basic questions

1 Look at the pictures and fill in the spaces.

(a)

There are (   ) 🥕 altogether.

Method I used: _____

Another method is: _____

(b) 🫐🫐🫐🫐🫐🫐🫐
🫐🫐🫐🫐🫐🫐🫐
🫐🫐🫐🫐🫐🫐🫐
🫐🫐🫐🫐🫐🫐🫐
🫐🫐

There are (   ) 🫐 altogether.

Method I used: _____

Another method is: _____

2 Find the greatest number that will fill in each bracket.

$6 \times (\quad) < 45$ $7 \times (\quad) < 40 - 5$ $27 + 8 > 6 \times (\quad)$

$(\quad) \times 9 < 32$ $(\quad) \times 5 < 4 \times 7$ $8 \times (\quad) < 20 + 27$

$22 = (\quad) \times 5 + (\quad)$ $63 = (\quad) \times 8 + (\quad)$

$53 = (\quad) \times 5 + (\quad)$ $21 = (\quad) \times 4 + (\quad)$

$69 = (\quad) \times 7 + (\quad)$ $25 = (\quad) \times 6 + (\quad)$

$59 = (\quad) \times 9 + (\quad)$ $67 = (\quad) \times 7 + (\quad)$

$47 = (\quad) \times 4 + (\quad)$

3 Fill in the brackets.

19 = 2 × (   ) + (   )   32 = 3 × (   ) + (   )

19 = 3 × (   ) + (   )   32 = 4 × (   ) + (   )

19 = 4 × (   ) + (   )   32 = 5 × (   ) + (   )

19 = 5 × (   ) + (   )   32 = 6 × (   ) + (   )

19 = 6 × (   ) + (   )   32 = 7 × (   ) + (   )

19 = 7 × (   ) + (   )   32 = 8 × (   ) + (   )

19 = 8 × (   ) + (   )   32 = 9 × (   ) + (   )

19 = 9 × (   ) + (   )   32 = 10 × (   ) + (   )

19 = 10 × (   ) + (   )   32 = 11 × (   ) + (   )

                                       32 = 12 × (   ) + (   )

4 Use the numbers below to write number sentences with both multiplication and addition.

| 15 | 26 | 6 | 2 | 4 | 3 | 7 | 1 |

Example: $6 × 4 + 2 = 26$

_____   _____

_____   _____

_____   _____

Challenge and extension question

5 A box of biscuits contains less than 40 biscuits. It is exactly enough to share equally with 6 children. If it is shared equally with 7 children, there is 1 biscuit left over.

There are (   ) biscuits in the box.

2.10 Division with a remainder

 Learning objective

Understand remainders in division as leftovers

Basic questions

1 Group the objects equally and write number sentences.
There are 22 cups in total.

(a)

There are (   ) groups.
There is/are (   ) left over.
Number sentence：_____

(b)

There are (   ) groups.
There is/are (   ) left over.
Number sentence：_____

2

Put the flowers into the 4 vases equally. Each vase has (   )
flowers. There are (   ) flowers left over.
Number sentence：_____

3

There are (   ) bells in a set. There are (   ) sets and (   )
bells left over.
Number sentence：_____

4 Calculate.

$17 \div 3 = \boxed{} \text{ r } \boxed{}$ $23 \div 7 = \boxed{} \text{ r } \boxed{}$ $38 \div 6 = \boxed{} \text{ r } \boxed{}$

$31 \div 4 = \boxed{} \text{ r } \boxed{}$ $64 \div 9 = \boxed{} \text{ r } \boxed{}$ $47 \div 8 = \boxed{} \text{ r } \boxed{}$

$41 \div 7 = \boxed{} \text{ r } \boxed{}$ $55 \div 8 = \boxed{} \text{ r } \boxed{}$ $92 \div 10 = \boxed{} \text{ r } \boxed{}$

5 Application problems.

(a) Mr Bruce gave a box of water to Kit, Tom, Ava and Maria equally. There were 9 bottles of water in the box. How many bottles did each child get?

Answer: _____

How many were left over?

Answer: _____

(b) A monkey gave her 7 baby monkeys some peaches. Each baby monkey got 6 peaches. There were 5 peaches left over. How many peaches were there altogether?

Answer: _____

(c) Mahmud has 50 ⫽ to make ⬡ without sharing edges. How many ⬡ can he make? How many ⫽ will be left over?

Answer: _____

Challenge and extension question

6 All the children in a class are grouped to take part in a school activity. If they are grouped in sevens, there is one child left over. If they are grouped in sixes, there is also one child left over. Given that there are fewer than 50 children in the class, the number of children in the class is (   ).

2.11 Calculation of division with a remainder (1)

 Learning objective

Solve division problems with remainders

 Basic questions

① Each box contains four pieces of ▱.

There are ( ) pieces of ▱ altogether. They are shared by ( ) children equally and each child gets ( ) pieces. There are ( ) pieces left over.

Number sentence: _____

② There are 45 🍎. 6 🍎 are put onto each plate. It is enough to fill in ( ) plates. There are ( ) 🍎 left over.

Number sentence: _____

③ Find the greatest number that will fill in each bracket.

7 × ( ) < 41   6 × ( ) < 35   3 × ( ) < 26

9 × ( ) < 38   ( ) × 5 < 43   ( ) × 2 < 20

( ) × 7 < 32   4 × ( ) < 43   ( ) × 8 < 65

4 Are these calculations correct? Put a √ for yes and a ✕ for no in each bracket.

(a) $46 \div 8 = 5 \text{ r } 6$　　(　)　　(b) $36 \div 6 = 5 \text{ r } 6$　　(　)

(c) $55 \div 7 = 7 \text{ r } 6$　　(　)　　(d) $44 \div 5 = 8 \text{ r } 4$　　(　)

(e) $80 \div 12 = 7 \text{ r } 4$　(　)　　(f) $99 \div 10 = 9 \text{ r } 9$　(　)

5 Write a number sentence for each question and calculate.

(a) There are 31 days in May and 7 days in a week. How many weeks plus how many days are there in May?

Number sentence：_____

(b) If each child gets 6 sweets, then how many children can share 50 sweets? How many sweets are left over?

Number sentence：_____

(c) If each coat needs 5 buttons to fit, then how many coats can 49 buttons fit? How many buttons are left over?

Number sentence：_____

Challenge and extension question

6 A class of twenty-six children plans to go boating.

Maximum capacity:
Big boat — 6 people
Small boat — 4 people

(a) If all the children take small boats, how many small boats will they need?

Answer：_____

(b) If all the children take big boats, how many big boats will they need?

Answer：_____

(c) Can you offer some other suggestions for renting the boats?

Answer：_____

2.12 Calculation of division with a remainder (2)

 Learning objective

Solve division problems with remainders

 Basic questions

1 Work these out mentally. Write the answers.

$37 \div 9 =$ $47 \div 5 =$ $43 \div 8 =$ $19 \div 7 =$

$69 \div 8 =$ $62 \div 7 =$ $26 \div 3 =$ $27 \div 6 =$

$9 \div 2 =$ $14 \div 4 =$ $95 \div 10 =$ $63 \div 6 =$

2 Fill in the brackets.

(   ) $\div 6 = 4$ r 4 (   ) $\div 7 = 6$ r 2

(   ) $\div 5 = 9$ r 1 (   ) $\div 9 = 3$ r 8

(   ) $\div 3 = 7$ r 2 (   ) $\div 7 = 7$ r 4

3 Fill in the brackets.

(a) Put 6 apples on each plate. 15 apples can be put on (   ) plates with (   ) apples left over.

Number sentence: (   ) $\div$ (   ) $=$ (   ) r (   )

(b) Some sweets were given to 8 children equally. After each child got 6 sweets, there were 4 sweets left over. How many sweets were there altogether?

Number sentence: (   ) $\times$ (   ) $+$ (   ) $=$ (   )

(c) 24 bananas were given to 5 monkeys equally, and each monkey got (   ) bananas, with (   ) bananas left over.

Number sentence: (   ) $\div$ (   ) $=$ (   ) r (   )

(d) In $\boxed{} \div 6 = 7$ r $\boxed{}$, the remainder could be (   ). The greatest possible remainder is (   ). When the remainder is the greatest, the dividend is (   ).

(e) From the number sentence $5 \times 7 + 5 = 40$, we can write another number sentence: $40 \div ($ $) = ($ $) \ r \ ($ $)$.

4 Use the number sentences of multiplication and addition to write number sentences of division with remainders.

$4 \times 3 + 1 = 13$ $4 \times 6 + 2 = 26$

$13 \div \square = 4 \ r \ \square$ $\square \div \square = \square \ r \ \square$

$13 \div \square = 3 \ r \ \square$ $\square \div \square = \square \ r \ \square$

5 Application problems.

(a) In a florist shop, a bouquet should have 6 flowers. How many bouquets can be made with 25 flowers? How many flowers will be left over?

Answer: _____

(b) 58 bananas are to be shared among 7 people equally. How many bananas will each person get? How many bananas will be left over?

Answer: _____

If each person should get 9 bananas, how many more bananas are needed?

Answer: _____

Challenge and extension question

6 In the list of numbers 1, 3, 5, 1, 3, 5, 1, 3, 5, ···, the 26th number is (   ). The sum of these 26 numbers is (   ).

2.13 Calculation of division with a remainder (3)

 Learning objective

Solve division problems with remainders

 Basic questions

1 Work these out mentally. Write the answers.

$5 \times 4 =$ $48 \div 6 =$ $28 \div 4 =$ $6 \times 9 =$

$16 \div 4 =$ $58 \div 8 =$ $4 \times 8 =$ $56 - 8 =$

$17 \div (\quad) = 8 \text{ r } 1$ $(\quad) \div 9 = 4 \text{ r } 2$ $(\quad) \div 6 = 8 \text{ r } 2$

$(\quad) \div 8 = 9 \text{ r } 7$ $(\quad) \div 7 = 4 \text{ r } 5$ $(\quad) \div 10 = 7 \text{ r } 1$

2 Find the remainder from each set of numbers and then work out the dividend.

(a) 5 6 7 8

   $(\quad) \div 6 = 6 \text{ r } (\quad)$

(b) 4 5 6 7

   $(\quad) \div 5 = 3 \text{ r } (\quad)$

(c) 3 4 5 6

   $(\quad) \div 4 = 7 \text{ r } (\quad)$

(d) 1 2 3 4

   $(\quad) \div 2 = 10 \text{ r } (\quad)$

3 Complete each calculation and then fill in the brackets.

(a) $\boxed{} \div 4 = 4 \text{ r } \bigcirc$

The greatest possible number in the $\boxed{}$ is (   ). The least possible number is (   ).

(b) $\boxed{} \div 9 = 3 \text{ r } \bigcirc$

The greatest possible number in the $\boxed{}$ is (   ). The least possible number is (   ).

4 Application problems.

(a) Jo's family has raised 3 ducks and 4 times as many chicks as ducks. How many chicks has the family raised?

Answer: _____

(b) The family has also raised 23 rabbits. A hutch can house 4 rabbits. How many hutches does the family need to house all the rabbits?

Answer: _____

(c) Jo has £50 to buy some kittens for her family. Each kitten costs £9. How many kittens can she buy?

Answer: _____

(d) The family has 5 black goldfish and 13 red goldfish. The number of red goldfish is (   ) more than (   ) times the number of black goldfish.

Challenge and extension questions

5 Fill in the boxes.

$35 \div \square = \square$ r 5 $57 \div \square = \square$ r 3

$35 \div \square = \square$ r 3 $57 \div \square = \square$ r 1

6 Six monkeys are sharing some peaches. If 5 more peaches are added, then each monkey can have 5 peaches. There are (   ) peaches.

Unit test 2

1 Work these out mentally. Write the answers.

$7 \times 7 =$ $8 + 15 =$ $6 \times 11 =$ $36 \div 3 =$

$35 + 5 =$ $72 \div 9 =$ $34 \div 8 =$ $88 \div 8 =$

$20 \div 5 =$ $0 \div 10 =$ $49 \div 7 =$ $100 - 36 + 36 =$

$27 = \boxed{} - 50$ $19 = \boxed{} \times 2 + \boxed{}$ $16 = \boxed{} \times 6 + \boxed{}$

2 Use the column method to calculate.

$33 + 38 =$ $65 - 38 =$ $64 + 36 - 17 =$ $85 - 67 + 39 =$

3 Write each number sentence and calculate.

(a) 45 is 29 more than what number?

Number sentence: _____

(b) What is the result of adding 12 twos together?

Number sentence: _____

(c) What is the result of multiplying 3 threes?

Number sentence: _____

(d) In a division calculation, both quotient and divisor are 8 and the remainder is 3. What is the dividend?

Number sentence: _____

4 Application problems.

(a) Look at each picture, write a number sentence and calculate.

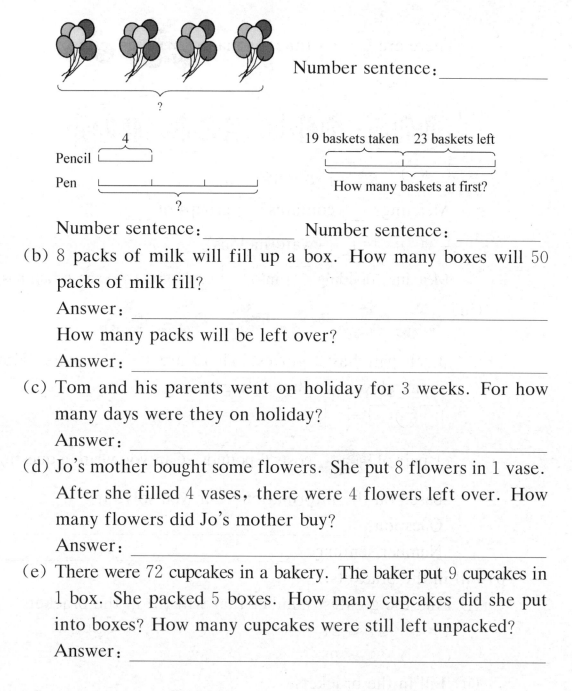

Number sentence:_____

Pencil ⎛ 4 ⎞

Pen ⎛_____⎞

?

19 baskets taken   23 baskets left

How many baskets at first?

Number sentence:_____   Number sentence:_____

(b) 8 packs of milk will fill up a box. How many boxes will 50 packs of milk fill?

Answer:_____

How many packs will be left over?

Answer:_____

(c) Tom and his parents went on holiday for 3 weeks. For how many days were they on holiday?

Answer:_____

(d) Jo's mother bought some flowers. She put 8 flowers in 1 vase. After she filled 4 vases, there were 4 flowers left over. How many flowers did Jo's mother buy?

Answer:_____

(e) There were 72 cupcakes in a bakery. The baker put 9 cupcakes in 1 box. She packed 5 boxes. How many cupcakes did she put into boxes? How many cupcakes were still left unpacked?

Answer:_____

5 Understand concepts.

(a) Look at each picture and fill in the missing numbers.

(i)

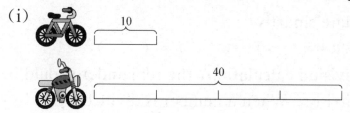

10

40

There are (   ) times as many 🏍 as 🚲.

(   ) ÷ (   ) = (   )

(ii)

□ ○ □ = □ (groups)

Meaning: □ contains □ groups of □.

□ ○ □ = □ (watermelons)

Meaning: dividing □ into □ equal groups, each group has □.

(iii)

Each pair has 2 gloves. There are (   ) pairs. How many gloves are there altogether?

□ ○ □ = □

1 pair of 🧤 costs 6 pounds. Can you write a question based on the information? Can you solve it?

Question: _____

Number sentence: _____

(b) Fill in the brackets.

(i) Find the greatest number that will fill in the brackets.

$4 \times ($ $) < 21$ $($ $) \times 5 < 46$

$($ $) \times 9 < 98$ $52 - ($ $) > 40$

(ii) Fill in the brackets.

$15 \times 2 = 5 \times ($ $)$ $12 \times ($ $) = ($ $) \times 24$

$2 + 2 + 2 + 4 = ($ $) \times ($ $)$

(iii) Calculate smartly.

$43 - 39 = ($ $) - ($ $) = ($ $)$

(iv) In a division calculation, the remainder should be (   ) than divisor. When a number is divided by 4, its quotient is 9 and the greatest possible remainder is (　　).

（v）When a number is divided by 9, the quotient is 4 and the remainder is 3. The number is (　　).

（vi）A pack contains fewer than 30 jellybeans. The jellybeans are exactly enough for 5 children to share equally. If they are shared equally by 6 children, there is 1 jellybean left over. There are (　　) jellybeans in the pack.

(c) True or false. (Put a $\checkmark$ for yes and a $\times$ for no in each bracket.)

（i）$33 \div 7 = 5$ r 2 ■■■■■■■■■■■■■■■■■ (　　)

（ii）If $\triangle \div 6 = \bigcirc$ r $\square$, then the greatest possible number of $\square$ is 5 ■■■■■■■■■■■■■■■■■■ (　　)

（iii）$12 \div 0 = 0$ ■■■■■■■■■■■■■■■■■■ (　　)

(d) Multiple choice questions. (Fill in each bracket with the letter of the correct answer.)

（i）$13 \div 3 = 4$ r 1 is read as (　　).

    A. 13 dividing by 3 equals 4.

    B. 13 divided by 3 equals 4 with a remainder of 1.

    C. 13 divided by 3 equals 4.

    D. 13 dividing by 3 equals 4 with a remainder of 1.

（ii）The quotient is 10, the divisor is 5, and the dividend is 50. The number sentence is (　　).

    A. $5 \times 10 = 50$ B. $10 \times 5 = 50$

    C. $50 \div 5 = 10$ D. $50 \div 10 = 5$

（iii）The number sentence with the same answer as 8×2 is (　　).

    A. $8 + 2$ B. 3×6 C. 2×9 D. 4×4

Chapter 3   Knowing numbers up to 1000

3.1   Knowing numbers up to 1000 (1)

 Learning objective

Read, write and partition numbers up to 1000

 Basic questions

1 Work these out mentally. Write the answers.

$7 \times 7 =$	$80 \div 10 =$	$45 - 18 =$	$50 \div 9 =$
$74 + 6 =$	$5 \times 8 =$	$44 + 13 =$	$54 \div 5 =$
$0 \div 3 =$	$10 \times 10 =$	$70 - 7 =$	$63 \div 9 =$

2 Look at each diagram and write the number. The first one has been done for you.

(a)

In numerals: <u>243</u>

In words: <u>two hundred and forty-three</u>

In numerals: _____

In words: _____

In numerals: _____

In words: _____

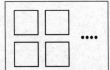

In numerals: _____

In words: _____

In numerals: _____

In words: _____

(b)

Hundreds	Tens	Ones
6	0	5

In numerals： _____

In words： _____

Hundreds	Tens	Ones
8	2	4

In numerals： _____

In words： _____

3 Fill in the brackets.

(a) 856 is made up of (   ) hundreds，(   ) tens and (   ) ones.

(b) Counting from the right in a 4-digit number，the first place is the (   ) place, the tens place is the (   ) place and the thousands place is the (   ) place.

(c) 707 is written in words as (   ). 7 in the ones place means (   ) ones. 7 in the hundreds place means (   ) hundreds. The difference between them is (   ).

(d) 4 hundreds and 3 ones make (   ). It is written in words as (   ).

4 Fill in the brackets.

$462 = ($ $) + ($ $) + ($ $)$

$1050 = ($ $) + ($ $) + ($ $) + ($ $)$

$788 = ($ $) + ($ $) + ($ $)$

$300 + 90 + 0 = ($ $)$ $800 + 8 = ($ $)$

Challenge and extension questions

5 1 duck ⇔ 3 fish   1 fish ⇔ 10 eggs   2 ducks ⇔ (   ) eggs

6 1 jug of water ⇔ 2 bottles of water

1 bottle of water ⇔ 4 cups of water

2 bottles of water ⇔ (   ) cups of water

1 jug of water ⇔ (   ) cups of water

3.2 Knowing numbers up to 1000 (2)

 Learning objective

Place value of numbers up to 1000

Basic questions

1 Work these out mentally. Write the answers.

$4 \times 7 \times 2 =$ $51 - 30 + 5 =$ $45 + 91 + 29 =$

$60 \div 6 + 29 =$ $4 \times 3 - 0 =$ $0 \times 4 + 62 =$

$51 + 37 - 59 =$ $1 \times 8 - 7 =$ $3 \times 0 + 48 =$

2 Look at the diagrams, and then write the numbers in numerals.

(a)

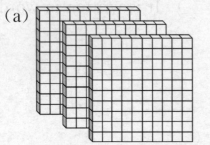

Written as: _____

(b)

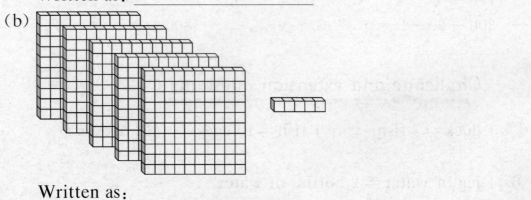

Written as: _____

3 Read the numbers, and then write them in words or in numerals.

635   In words: _____

302 In words: _____

Nine hundred and thirty-six In numerals: _____

1000 In words: _____

Four hundred In numerals: _____

4 Fill in the brackets.

(a) Four hundred and eight is written in numerals as (   ). It is a (   )-digit number. It consists of (   ) hundreds and (   ) ones.

(b) The number consisting of 6 tens and 4 hundreds is (   ).

(c) 10 one hundreds is (   ). (   ) one hundreds is 500.

(d) The numbers that come before and after 300 are (   ) and (   ) respectively.

(e) There are (   ) tens in 470.

5 Draw diagrams to represent numbers and then write them in numerals. The first one has been done for you.

(a) One hundred and eighty-seven

Draw: ☐ ≡ ≡ •••••• .   Written as: 187

(b) Six hundred and six

Draw: _____ .   Written as: _____

(c) Two hundred and eighty

Draw: _____ .   Written as: _____

Challenge and extension question

6 Three numbers 4, 0 and 2 can be used to make (   ) three-digit numbers. Write these numbers and put them in order starting from the greatest, using > to link them.

Answer: _____

3.3   Number lines (in thousands) (1)

Learning objective

Compare and order numbers up to 1000

Basic questions

1 Complete these questions about number lines.

(a) Mark the numbers on the number line.

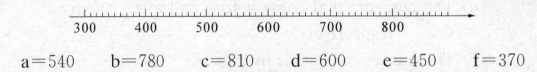

a=540   b=780   c=810   d=600   e=450   f=370

(b) Fill in the bracket with the number that each letter stands for.

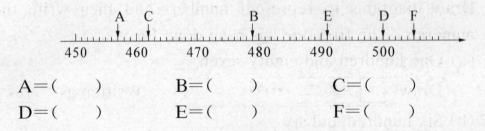

A=(   )   B=(   )   C=(   )

D=(   )   E=(   )   F=(   )

2 Fill in the brackets with numbers based on the given information.

(a) Write the numbers that come before and after each number.

(   ), 278, (   ) (   ), 999, (   ) (   ), 406, (   )

(b) Write the whole tens that come before and after each number.

(   ), 390, (   ) (   ), 455, (   ) (   ), 789, (   )

(c) Write the whole hundreds that come before and after each number.

(   ), 657, (   ) (   ), 405, (   ) (   ), 790, (   )

3 Count and complete the number patterns.

(a) 567, 568, 569, (   ), (   )

(b) 350, 370, 390, (　　), (　　), 450

(c) 743, 742, 741, (　　), (　　)

(d) 250, (　　), (　　), 550, 650, 750.

4　Choose suitable numbers in the list below to fill in the blanks.

439　501　92　888　654　499　328　1000

(a) The numbers greater than 400 but less than 500 are ＿＿＿＿＿.

(b) The number that is 111 less than 999 is ＿＿＿＿＿.

(c) The numbers that come before and after 500 are ＿＿＿＿＿.

(d) Write the above numbers in order starting from the greatest.

＿＿＿＿＿＿＿＿＿＿＿＿＿＿＿＿＿＿＿＿＿＿＿＿＿

5　Write the numbers.

(a) Write the numbers greater than 498 but less than 505.

＿＿＿＿＿＿＿＿＿＿＿＿＿＿＿＿＿＿＿＿＿＿＿＿＿

(b) Write the whole hundreds less than 900.

＿＿＿＿＿＿＿＿＿＿＿＿＿＿＿＿＿＿＿＿＿＿＿＿＿

(c) Write all the three-digit numbers that are less than 200 and have the same digit in the ones place and in the tens place.

＿＿＿＿＿＿＿＿＿＿＿＿＿＿＿＿＿＿＿＿＿＿＿＿＿

Challenge and extension questions

6　In some three-digit numbers, the sum of the three digits is 15 and the digit in the hundreds place is twice the digit in the ones place. These three-digit numbers are: (　　　　　　).

7　When you write numbers from 200 to 300, you need to write the digits 1 (　　) times, 2 (　　) times and 0 (　　) times.

3.4　Number lines (in thousands) (2)

Learning objective

Compare and order numbers up to 1000

Basic questions

1 Complete these questions about number lines.

560	570	580	590	600	610

(a) Mark the following numbers on the number line.

$a = 587$ $b = 565$ $c = 599$

$d = 571$ $e = 602$ $f = 618$

(b) Make up the whole tens.

$a + (\quad) = 590$ $b + (\quad) = 570$ $c - (\quad) = 590$

$d - (\quad) = 570$ $e + (\quad) = 610$ $f - (\quad) = 610$

(c) Make up the whole hundreds.

$a + (\quad) = 600$ $b - (\quad) = 500$ $c + (\quad) = 600$

$d - (\quad) = 500$ $e + (\quad) = 700$ $f - (\quad) = 600$

(d) Put the 6 numbers a, b, c, d, e and f in order, starting from the smallest.

$(\quad) < (\quad) < (\quad) < (\quad) < (\quad) < (\quad)$

2 Count and complete the number patterns.

(a) _____ , _____ 290, 285, _____ , _____

(b) 486, 488, _____ , _____

(c) 123, 223, 323, _____ , _____ , _____

3 Write the numbers in order.

(a) Start with the greatest: 175　715　517　157　751　117

(b) Start with the least: 869　886　689　668　969　898

_____

(c) From the greatest to the least: all the three-digit numbers with 7 in the ones place and 6 in the tens place.

_____

4 Fill in the $\bigcirc$ with $>$, $<$ or $=$.

428 $\bigcirc$ 482　　　　789 $\bigcirc$ 787　　　　543 $\bigcirc$ 453

603 $\bigcirc$ 630　　　　1000 $\bigcirc$ 999　　　135 $\bigcirc$ 125

155 $\bigcirc$ 205　　　　299 $\bigcirc$ 301　　　438 $\bigcirc$ 400 + 30 + 8

5 Find the greatest number that will fill in each box.

$\square$ 65 < 655　　　7 $\square$ 8 > 778　　　453 < 4 $\square$ 3

321 > $\square$ 21　　　642 > $\square$ 43　　　795 < 79 $\square$

Challenge and extension questions

6 Fill in the boxes with the same number so the subtraction is correct.

$$
\begin{array}{r}
1\ \ 9\ \ 8 \\
-\ \ \square\ \square \\
\hline
\square\ \square
\end{array}
$$

7 Write a suitable one-digit number in each of the $\square$ and $\bigcirc$ in 70 ÷ $\square$ = $\bigcirc$ r 6 so that the number sentence is correct. Write out the number sentence(s).

_____

_____

3.5 Fun with the place value chart (1)

Learning objective

Place value of numbers up to 1000

Basic questions

1 Look at the diagrams and write the numbers.

Hundreds	Tens	Ones
●●●● ●●●	●●●	●●●●

In words: _____
In numerals: _____

Hundreds	Tens	Ones
●●●●	●●●	

In words: _____
In numerals: _____

Hundreds	Tens	Ones
●●●		●

In words: _____
In numerals: _____

Hundreds	Tens	Ones
●●●●		

In words: _____
In numerals: _____

2 Draw dots in the place value chart to represent each number given.

507

Hundreds	Tens	Ones

800

Hundreds	Tens	Ones

3 Mary has drawn the dots representing 264 in the place value chart below. John adds one more dot. What could be the new number?

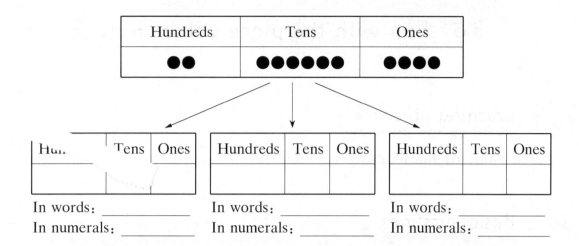

Hundreds	Tens	Ones
●●	●●●●●●	●●●●

Hu...	Tens	Ones

In words: _____
In numerals: _____

Hundreds	Tens	Ones

In words: _____
In numerals: _____

Hundreds	Tens	Ones

In words: _____
In numerals: _____

Challenge and extension questions

4 Peter folded a piece of paper in half three times. He then drew a flower in the centre and cut it out. Peter cut out (   ) flowers in the paper.

5 After drinking half a cup of milk, Jo filled up the cup with water. She then drank half of the contents of the cup again. After that, she filled up the cup with water for a second time. She then drank the whole of the contents of the cup. In total, Jo drank (   ) cup(s) of milk and (   ) cup(s) of water.

3.6 Fun with the place value chart (2)

 Learning objective

Place value of numbers up to 1000

Basic questions

1. Draw three dots in each place value chart to represent six different three-digit numbers.

Hundreds	Tens	Ones

In words: _____
In numerals: _____

Hundreds	Tens	Ones

In words: _____
In numerals: _____

Hundreds	Tens	Ones

In words: _____
In numerals: _____

Hundreds	Tens	Ones

In words: _____
In numerals: _____

Hundreds	Tens	Ones

In words: _____
In numerals: _____

Hundreds	Tens	Ones

In words: _____
In numerals: _____

2. Draw dots in the first place value chart to represent 153. Then, in each place value chart below, move one dot into another column and write the number.

Hundreds	Tens	Ones

Hundreds	Tens	Ones

In words: _____
In numerals: _____

Hundreds	Tens	Ones

In words: _____
In numerals: _____

Hundreds	Tens	Ones

In words: _____
In numerals: _____

Hundreds	Tens	Ones

In words: _____
In numerals: _____

Hundreds	Tens	Ones

In words: _____
In numerals: _____

Hundreds	Tens	Ones

In words: _____
In numerals: _____

❸ Fill in the brackets.

643 = (   ) + (   ) + (   )   300 + 30 + 8 = (   )
302 = (   ) + (   ) + (   )   900 + 0 + 9 = (   )

Challenge and extension questions

❹ A group of children form a line for a running race. Lily is in the twelfth place counting from the start. Tim is in the twelfth place counting from the end. Lily is exactly in front of Tim. There are (   ) children in total.

❺ A book has 40 pages. If a tree leaf is put in every three pages starting from the first page, it has (   ) tree leaves in total.

Unit test 3

1 Work these out mentally. Write the answers.

$7 \times 5 =$ $1000 - 960 =$ $3 \times 9 =$ $72 \div 8 =$

$45 \div 9 =$ $4 \times 8 =$ $640 + 40 =$ $43 - 12 =$

$860 - 50 =$ $55 + 24 =$ $83 - 8 =$ $370 - 300 =$

2 Write the numbers in words and make a drawing to represent them.

        165   608

In words: _____   In words: _____

Drawing: _____   Drawing: _____

3 Look at the diagrams and write the numbers.

Thousands	Hundreds	Tens	Ones
●			

In words: _____   In words: _____

In numerals: _____   In numerals: _____

4 Write each number sentence and calculate.

(a) How much more is the sum of 8 twos than 10?

     Number sentence: _____

(b) Add 27 to the difference between 31 and 15. How much is it?

     Number sentence: _____

(c) Both addends are 7. What is the sum?

     Number sentence: _____

5 Fill in the brackets.

(a) The even numbers that come before and after 700 are (   )

     and (   ).

(b) Complete these questions about number lines.

```
          a       b                    c    e          d
   |lunuu|lunuu|lun|uuu|lunuu|lunuu|lunu|luuu|lunuu|lun|lunuu|lunuu| →
   450              500              550              600
```

(i) Mark 456, 580, 489, 558 and 520 on the number line.

(ii) Write the number each letter represents.

a=(   ) b=(   ) c=(   ) d=(   ) e=(   )

(c) 247 is a (   )-digit number. The place with the greatest value is the (   ) place. The number is made up of (   ) hundreds, (   ) tens and (   ) ones.

(d) The greatest two-digit number is (   ). The number which is 100 greater than it is (   ).

(e) 387+(   )=400; 650−(   )=600; (   )+ 258=1000

(f) 2 hundreds and 18 tens make (   ).

(g) Arrange the numbers 45, 405, 380, 1000, 806 and 968 in order starting from the greatest: (   )

6 True or false.

(a) The place with the greater value in 65 is in the tens place, therefore it is a ten-digit number. (   )

(b) 5 hundreds and 4 ones make 504. (   )

(c) There are 37 tens in 370. (   )

(d) To make $\square$×4<31 true, the $\square$ can be filled in with any of the seven numbers 1, 2, 3, 4, 5, 6 and 7. (   )

7 Multiple choice questions.

(a) The place with the greatest value in a three-digit number is the (   ).

A. ones place   B. tens place

C. hundreds place   D. thousands place

(b) Using $\square$ to represent hundreds and ● to represent ones,

□□□□●●●●●● represents the number (   ).

A. 46   B. 460   C. 604   D. 406

(c) The whole tens that come before and after 786 are (   ).

A. 785 and 787   B. 780 and 790

C. 700 and 800   D. 770 and 790

(d) No matter how one more dot is added into the place value chart below, the number represented cannot be (   ).

Hundreds	Tens	Ones
●●	●●●	

A. 330   B. 240   C. 231   D. 241

8 A class in Year 3 has 30 children. For a school reading program, the class is divided into 6 groups. Each group receives 9 books. How many books does the class receive in total?

9 How many legs do 8 chicks and 3 rabbits have in total?

10 A car can seat 4 children. How many cars are needed for 30 children?

11 A sports club has 34 footballs, 18 fewer than the volleyballs. There are 28 more basketballs than volleyballs. How many volleyballs does the club have? How many basketballs are there?

Chapter 4 Statistics (Ⅱ)

4.1 From statistical table to bar chart

 Learning objective

Interpret and represent data using tables and bar charts

 Basic questions

1 60 children are divided into 3 groups for three different tasks. Group A has 20 children，Group B has 30 children and Group C has 10 children. Present this information by completing the following.

(a) A statistics table

	Group A	Group B	Group C
Number of children			

(b) A pictogram

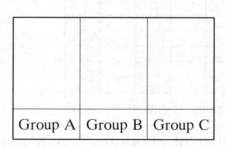

Each ◯ stands for 10 children.

(c) A block diagram

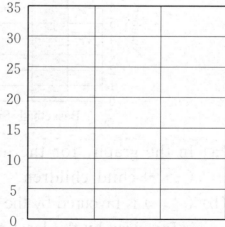

Each cell stands for 5 children.

2 Read the bar chart and complete the statistical table.

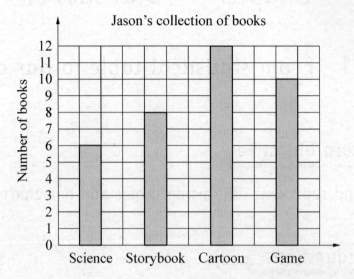

Type of book	Science	Storybook	Cartoon	Game
Number of books				

3 Fill in the brackets based on the bar chart. (Each child chose one favourite sport only.)

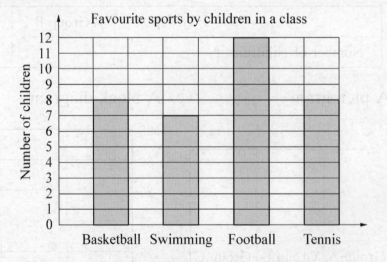

(a) In the graph, for the number of children, 1 unit represents ( ) child/children.

(b) ( ) is favoured by the greatest number of children and ( ) is favoured by the least number of children. The difference is ( ) children.

（c）Two sports，（   ）and（   ），were equally favoured in the class.

（d）There are（   ）children in total in the class.

Challenge and extension question

4　How many of the following items of stationery do you have? Find out and complete the table. Then use another suitable statistical tool you have learned to present the data.

Type	Quantity
pencil	
eraser	
coloured pen	
exercise book	

4.2　Bar chart (1)

 Learning objective

Interpret and represent data using bar charts

 Basic questions

1 Read the bar chart and fill in the brackets.

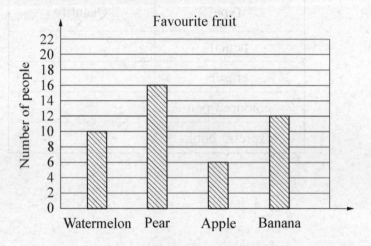

(a) In the graph, for the number of people, 1 unit represents
（　　）people.

(b) Pear is （　　）people's favourite fruit while banana is （　　）
people's favourite fruit.

(c) There are （　　）more people choosing watermelon than
apple as their favourite fruit.

(d) There are （　　）people in total choosing these as their
favourite fruit.

(e) There are （　　）times as many people choosing banana as
their favourite fruit as those choosing apple.

2 Read the bar chart and fill in the brackets. （Each child chose one
favourite toy only.）

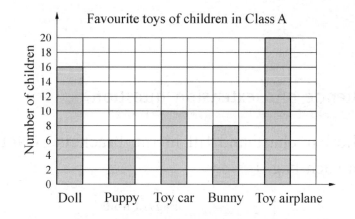

Type	doll	puppy	toy car	bunny	toy airplane
Number of children					

(a) Complete the table.

(b) The toy favoured by the greatest number of children is (　　), and that by the least number of children is (　　). The difference is (　　) children.

(c) Based on the data above, there are (　　) children in total in Class A.

3 Joan did a survey on the number of children taking part in PE activities and presented the data in the table below. Complete a bar chart based on the data.

Type	rope skipping	benchball	football	running
Number of children	6	11	8	13

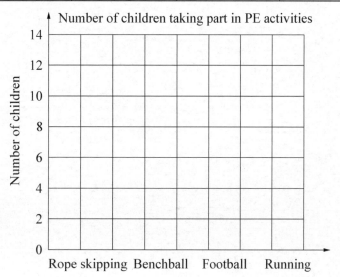

Challenge and extension question

4 Read the bar chart and fill in the brackets. (Note: there are 4 fruits in each bag.)

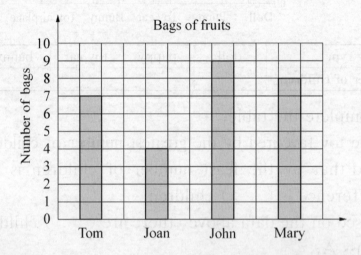

(a) (   ) has 2 times as many bags of fruits as (   ).

(b) For the 4 children to have the same number of bags of fruits, each one should have (   ) bags.

(c) Tom has (   ) fewer fruits than John.

4.3 Bar chart (2)

Learning objective

Interpret and represent data using tables, pictograms and bar charts

Basic questions

1. The pictogram shows information about the ages of the children participating in a school activity.

| 6 | 7 | 8 | 9 | 10 | 11 |

Each ⟨figure⟩ stands for 2 children.

(a) How many children are aged 9? How many are younger than 9? How many are older than 9?

    Answers: _____

(b) How many children in total participate in the school activity?

    Answer: _____

(c) Complete a bar chart based on the information given in the pictogram.

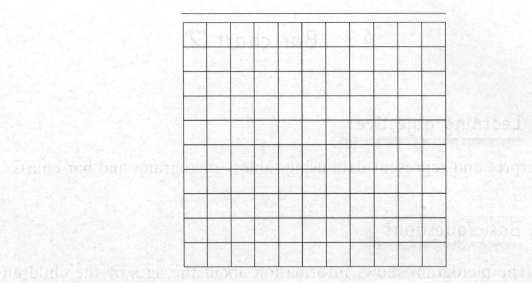

2 In the school sports games, John, Tom, Joan, Mary and Lily had a competition in ball bouncing. Their results are recorded in the table below.

Results of ball bouncing by five children

Name	John	Tom	Joan	Mary	Lily
Number of times	40	25	50	45	35

(a) Read the results and put the five children in order, starting from the child who won first place.

_____

(b) Complete a bar chart based on the table.

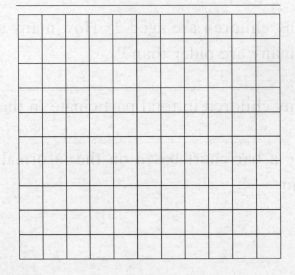

Challenge and extension question

3 Read the bar chart and fill in the brackets. (Each child takes part in one activity only.)

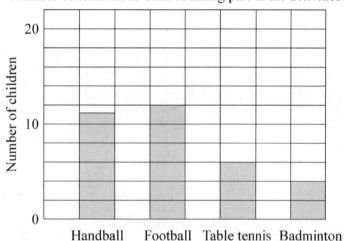

Number of children in Class A taking part in the activities

(a) In the graph, for the number of children, 1 unit represents ( ) child/children.

(b) The activity attracting the greatest number of participants is ( ) and that attracting the least number of participants is ( ).

(c) There are ( ) children taking part in all the activities in Class A.

(d) The difference between the number of children taking part in handball and that in football is ( ).

Unit test 4

1 In the bar charts below, what does 1 cell stand for? What does each bar stand for?

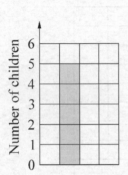 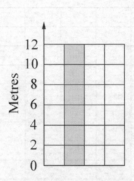 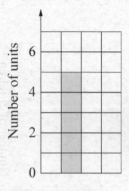

1 cell stands for ____   1 cell stands for ____   1 cell stands for ____

The bar stands for ____   The bar stands for ____   The bar stands for ____

2 The bar chart shows the number of people using different ways to go to work in one company. Fill in the brackets based on the bar chart.

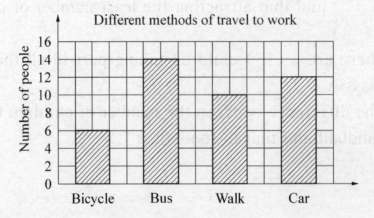

(a) In the graph, 1 cell stands for ( ) person(s).

(b) The largest number of people go to work in the company by ( ). The number is ( ). The fewest number of people go to work by ( ). The number is ( ).

(c) There are (　　　) people taking bus or car to go to work.

(d) There are (　　　) people in total working in the company.

3 Look at the bar chart.

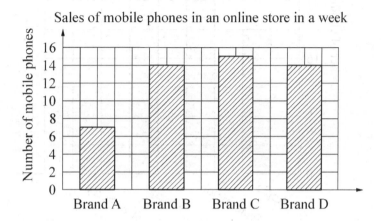

(a) Complete the table based on the bar chart.

Brand	Brand A	Brand B	Brand C	Brand D
Number of mobile phones sold				

(b) Based on the sales recorded, the most popular brand is (　　　) and the least popular is (　　　).

(c) Two brands, (　　　) and (　　　), are equally popular according to the sales in the week.

(d) The store sold (　　　) mobile phones of the four brands in the week.

4 The bar chart below shows the favourite fruit of children in a school.

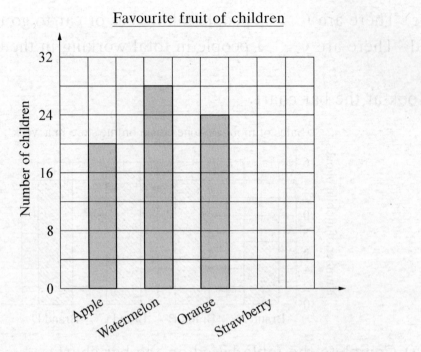

Favourite fruit of children

(a) In the graph, 1 unit of the number of children represents (   ) child/children. There are (   ) children whose favourite fruit is watermelon. (   ) fewer children favour apple than orange.

(b) 14 children's favourite fruit is strawberry. Complete the bar chart to show this information.

(c) Write your own question based on the bar chart and give the answer.

_____

_____

_____

Chapter 5   Introduction to time (Ⅲ)

5.1   Second and minute

 Learning objective

Understand second and minute as units of time

Basic questions

1 Complete the sentences.

(a) There are _____ seconds in a minute.

(b) There are _____ minutes in an hour.

(c) There are _____ seconds in half a minute.

(d) There are _____ seconds in 10 minutes.

2 Draw lines to match the times.

| 3:05 | 8:26 | 4:59 | 11:11 |

3 Fill in each bracket with a suitable unit of time.

(a) It took Tom 48 (   ) to swim 50 metres.

(b) Anya practises playing the piano 1 (   ) every day.

(c) Ahmed's father works 8 (   ) a day.

(d) The children have a 50 (   ) lunch break.

4 Converting times in different units.

$\frac{1}{2}$ hour= _____ minutes   5 minutes= _____ seconds

$\frac{3}{4}$ hours= _____ minutes   120 seconds= _____ minutes

1 hour 40 minutes= _____ minutes

2 minutes 30 seconds= _____ seconds

90 seconds= _____ minute _____ seconds

100 minutes= _____ hour _____ minutes

5 Try the following activities and record the results.
(a) I can read (   ) English words in 1 minute.
(b) I can skip with a rope (   ) times in 1 minute.
(c) It takes me (   ) seconds to walk 50 metres.
(d) My heart beats (   ) times in 10 seconds.

Challenge and extension questions

6 Complete the sentences with the correct times. (Hint: you may use a clock face to help you.)
(a) It is now 2:30. After 1 hour, it is _____.
(b) It is now 5:35. After 2 hours, it is _____.
(c) It is now 11:28. After 5 minutes, it is _____.
(d) It is now 6:17. After 1 hour and 30 minutes, it is _____.

7 To the nearest minute, the time shown on the clock face on the right is _____. Give your reason. (Hint: think of the position of the second hand.)
Reason: _____

5.2　Times on 12-hour and 24-hour clock and in Roman numerals

Learning objective

Read times in Roman numerals and convert between 12-hour and 24-hour times

Basic questions

1 Fill in the brackets.

(a) There are (　　) hours in a day.

(b) There are (　　) hours in half a day.

(c) The time at noon is (　　) o'clock.

(d) In a day, the time from midnight to noon is called (　　) or a. m.

(e) The time from noon to midnight is called (　　) or p. m.

2 What number does each Roman numeral represent? The first one has been done for you.

IX＝9　　　I＝　　　X＝　　　II＝　　　VI＝　　　XI＝
XII＝　　　VII＝　　III＝　　　V＝　　　IV＝　　VIII＝

3 Read each clock and write the time in digits.

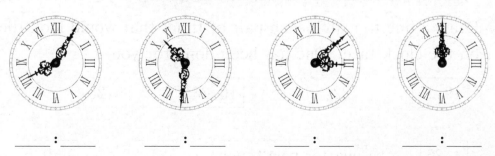

＿＿：＿＿　　　＿＿：＿＿　　　＿＿：＿＿　　　＿＿：＿＿

4 Complete the table for converting 12-hour time to 24-hour time. The first one has been done for you.

12-hour time	24-hour time
3:03 a.m.	03:03
8:00 a.m.	
	13:36
	23:58
12:00 midnight	

5 Read and write the time on 24-hour clocks.

___:___ or ___:___   ___:___ or ___:___   ___:___ or ___:___

6 The traffic road sign shows that the road is closed to all traffic from _____ to _____ in the morning and from _____ to _____ in the afternoon. The road is closed to traffic for _____ hours in a day.

7:30~10:30
16:30~19:30

 Challenge and extension question

7 Draw a line to match each pair of times that would look the same on the clock face. One has been done for you.

| 19:15 | 22:30 | 16:25 | 9:25 |

| 4:25 | a quarter past seven | 21:25 | half past ten |

5.3 Leap years and common years

Learning objective

Know the number of days in each leap year and common year

Basic questions

1. True or false? Put a √ for true and a × for false in each bracket.
   (a) One day always has 24 hours.   (   )
   (b) One week always has 7 days.   (   )
   (c) One month always has 30 days.   (   )
   (d) One year always has 12 months.   (   )
   (e) One year always has 365 days.   (   )

2. Check the calendar for 2016 and complete the table.

Month	Jan	Feb	Mar	Apr	May	Jun	Jul	Aug	Sept	Oct	Nov	Dec
Number of days												

3. Use the information in the table above to fill in the brackets.
   (a) There are (   ) days in April. The months that have the same number of days as April are (   ).
   (b) Christmas Day is on the (   ) of (   ). The months that have the same number of days as that month are (   ).
   (c) The month that has the fewest days is (   ). There are (   ) days in that month.
   (d) There are (   ) days in 2016.

4 Using a print or online calendar, find the number of days in each year and the number of days in February for any 10 consecutive years.

Year	Number of days in the year	Number of days in February

5 Use the information in the table above to fill in the brackets.

(a) There are (   ) days in most of the months of February. These years are called common years.

(b) There are (   ) days in some of the months of February. These years are called leap years.

(c) A common year has (   ) days. A leap year has (   ) days.

(d) 2016 is a leap year. The next two leap years are (   ) and (   ).

Challenge and extension question

6 Alvin is a primary school child. He said: "I have only had a birthday three times, including the day I was born." On which day do you think he was born?

5.4   Calculating the duration of time

 Learning objective

Compare the duration of events

Basic questions

1. Fill in the ○ with >, < or =.

   1 hour ○ 60 seconds   2 minutes ○ 100 seconds

   2 days ○ 20 hours   3 hours ○ 200 minutes

   1 month ○ 27 days   52 weeks ○ 1 year

2. Fill in the brackets.
   (a) Mary left home at 9:00 a.m. and came back at 1:00 p.m. She was away for (   ) hours.
   (b) Lily began her homework at 6:00 p.m. and finished at 6:45 p.m. She spent (   ) minutes doing her homework.
   (c) A party started at 19:30 and ended at 21:40. It lasted (   ) hours and (   ) minutes.
   (d) A volleyball match started at 19:30 and lasted 155 minutes. It ended at (   ).

3. The opening hours for a store on weekdays are shown below.
   (a) The superstore opens at (   ) in the morning and closes at (   ) in the evening.
   (b) The superstore is open for (   ) hours and (   ) minutes on weekdays.

   ABC Superstore

   8:30~21:00

(c) It takes Anna 20 minutes to go from her office to the superstore. If she leaves the office for the superstore at 8 p.m., does she still have time to do shopping? (   ) If so, for how long? (   )

4 The 2012 Summer Olympics was held in London from 27 July 2012 to 12 August 2012. What was the duration of the event? (   )

5 A local computer store had three storewide promotional sales in the first half of 2015. The dates are given below.

First promotion	23/02/2015 till 02/03/2015
Second promotion	23/03/2015 till 01/04/2015
Third promotion	25/04/2015 till 03/05/2015

(a) Which promotion had the longest period of time? How long was it? (   )

(b) Which promotion had the shortest period of time? How long was it? (   )

(c) For how many days did the store have a storewide promotion in the first half of 2015? (   )

Challenge and extension question

6 A popular drama series was broadcast from Thursday 7 March 2013 to 4 April 2013. Two episodes of the series were broadcast every day from Monday to Thursday and one episode was broadcast on Saturday and Sunday. There was no broadcasting on Friday. The drama series had (   ) episodes and was broadcast for (   ) days.

Unit test 5

1 Use digits and a colon to write the time shown on each clock face below to the nearest minute.

2 Draw the minute hand and hour hand on each clock face to show the time given.

    5:30   18:03   12:25   21:48

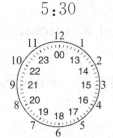   

3 Fill in the brackets.

2 minutes＝(   ) seconds   2 days＝(   ) hours

1 minute and 10 seconds＝(   ) seconds

100 seconds＝(   ) minute and (   ) seconds

1 hour and 30 minutes＝(   ) minutes

85 minutes＝(   ) hour and (   ) minutes

4 Fill in the ◯ with ＞, ＜ or ＝.

60 seconds ◯ 1 minute   1 minute and 40 seconds ◯ 100 seconds

100 minutes ◯ 1 hour   1 and a half days ◯ 30 hours

20 hours ◯ 1 day   1 and a quarter hours ◯ 90 minutes

5 True or false.

(a) There are always 183 days in the first half of a year. (   )

(b) Compared with all the other months, February has the least number of days.   (   )

(c) John works 35 hours every week. He works 140 hours in a month.   (   )

(d) If a month has 31 days, then the following month must have 30 days.   (   )

6 Fill in the brackets.

(a) Tom left school at 3:13 p.m. After 25 minutes he arrived home. He reached home at (   ).

(b) The duration of a flight from City A to City B was 2 hours. It arrived in City B at 1:40 p.m. The flight took off from City A at (   ).

(c) The football match ended at 20:00. It lasted 90 minutes. The football match started at (   ).

(d) A toy shop sold 7 toy cars each day. It sold (   ) toy cars in total from 30 August to 10 September.

7 John and his family went for holiday. They spent 2 days fewer than 2 weeks. How many days did they spend on holiday?

Answer: _____

8 Write the time shown on each clock face in the boxes below. Then fill in each bracket with the duration from the time shown on one clock face to the time shown on the next.

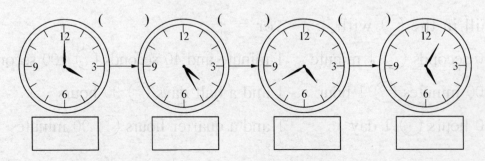

83

Chapter 6   Consolidation and enhancement

6.1   5 threes plus 3 threes equals 8 threes

 Learning objective

Solve problems involving multiplication and addition

 Basic questions

1 Look at the pictures and complete the number sentences.
   (a) How many apples and pears are there altogether?

$$\square\times3+\square\times3=\square\times3=\square$$

   (b) How many pineapples and apples are there altogether?

$$\square\times\square+\square\times\square=\square\times\square=\square$$

2 Complete the table.

	1	2	3	4	5	6	7	8	9	10
2 times										
4 times										
6 times										

2 times a number plus 4 times the same number equals (   ) times this number.

$$2\times\square+4\times\square=\square\times\square$$

3 Fill in the brackets.

$3 \times 6 + 5 \times 6 = ($ 　 $) \times 6 = ($ 　 $)$

$3 \times 4 + 6 \times 4 = ($ 　 $) \times 4 = ($ 　 $)$

$8 \times 2 + 2 \times 2 = 10 \times ($ 　 $) = ($ 　 $)$

$7 \times 7 + 2 \times 7 = 7 \times ($ 　 $) = ($ 　 $)$

4 Work these out mentally. Write the answers.

$4 \times 8 + 2 \times 8 = ($ 　 $)$ 　　　　 $5 \times 7 + 4 \times 7 = ($ 　 $)$

$5 \times 9 + 5 \times 9 = ($ 　 $)$ 　　　　 $6 \times 2 + 3 \times 2 = ($ 　 $)$

5 Think carefully. What number can you fill in each bracket?

$8 \times 3 + ($ 　 $) \times 3 = 9 \times 3$ 　　　 $4 \times 6 + ($ 　 $) \times 6 = 6 \times 6$

$($ 　 $) \times 5 + 2 \times 5 = 5 \times 5$ 　　　 $2 \times ($ 　 $) + 6 \times ($ 　 $) = 8 \times 7$

6 Each pen costs £9. Tom bought 2 pens and Joan bought 3 pens. How much did they pay in total?

Answer: _____

Challenge and extension questions

7 Think carefully and then fill in the brackets.

$4 \times 8 + 8 = ($ 　 $) \times 8$ 　　　　　　 $6 \times 5 + ($ 　 $) = 7 \times 5$

8 Use different ways to express 9×5.

$9 \times 5 = ($ 　 $) \times ($ 　 $) + ($ 　 $) \times ($ 　 $)$

$9 \times 5 = ($ 　 $) \times ($ 　 $) + ($ 　 $) \times ($ 　 $)$

$9 \times 5 = ($ 　 $) \times ($ 　 $) + ($ 　 $) \times ($ 　 $)$

$9 \times 5 = ($ 　 $) \times ($ 　 $) + ($ 　 $) \times ($ 　 $)$

$9 \times 5 = ($ 　 $) \times ($ 　 $) + ($ 　 $) \times ($ 　 $) + ($ 　 $) \times ($ 　 $)$

6.2　5 threes minus 3 threes equals 2 threes

 Learning objective

Solve problems involving multiplication and subtraction

 Basic questions

1 Look at the pictures，write number sentences and then calculate.

(a) How many more pineapples are there than apples?

$$\boxed{}\times 2 - \boxed{}\times 2 = \boxed{}\times 2 = \boxed{}$$

(b) How many are left over?

$$\boxed{}\times\boxed{} - \boxed{}\times\boxed{} = \boxed{}\times\boxed{} = \boxed{}$$

2 Complete the table and then fill in the answers below.

	1	2	3	4	5	6	7	8	9	10
9 times										
5 times										
4 times										

9 times a number minus 5 times the same number equals (　　) times this number.

$$9\times\boxed{} - 5\times\boxed{} = \boxed{}\times\boxed{}$$

3 Fill in the brackets.

$8 \times 6 - 5 \times 6 = ($ $) \times 6 = ($ $)$

$7 \times 4 - 6 \times 4 = 4 \times ($ $) = ($ $)$

$5 \times 9 - 5 \times 6 = 5 \times ($ $) = ($ $)$

$5 \times 7 - 2 \times 7 = ($ $) \times ($ $) = ($ $)$

$9 \times 6 - 4 \times ($ $) = ($ $) \times 6 = ($ $)$

4 Work these out mentally. Write the answers.

$12 \times 8 - 10 \times 8 = ($ $)$ $\qquad 15 \times 7 - 9 \times 7 = ($ $)$

$18 \times 9 - 9 \times 9 = ($ $)$ $\qquad 16 \times 2 - 7 \times 2 = ($ $)$

5 Think carefully and fill in the brackets.

$8 \times 3 - ($ $) \times 3 = 6 \times 3$ $\quad 12 \times 6 - ($ $) \times 6 = 9 \times 6$

$($ $) \times 5 - 6 \times 5 = 4 \times 5$ $\quad 10 \times ($ $) - 6 \times ($ $) = ($ $) \times 7$

6 Each pen costs £9. Tom bought 8 pens and Joan bought 3 pens. How much more did Tom pay than Joan?

Answer: _____

Challenge and extension questions

7 Think carefully and then fill in the brackets.

$8 \times 8 - 8 = ($ $) \times ($ $)$ $\qquad 8 \times 5 = 12 \times 5 - ($ $) \times ($ $)$

$8 \times 7 - 2 \times 7 - 4 \times 7 = 7 \times ($ $)$

$2 \times 2 = 9 \times 2 - 4 \times ($ $) - ($ $) \times ($ $)$

8 Use different ways to express 3×6.

$3 \times 6 = ($ $) \times ($ $) - ($ $) \times ($ $)$

$3 \times 6 = ($ $) \times ($ $) - ($ $) \times ($ $)$

$3 \times 6 = ($ $) \times ($ $) - ($ $) \times ($ $)$

$3 \times 6 = ($ $) \times ($ $) - ($ $) \times ($ $) - ($ $) \times ($ $)$

6.3　Multiplication and division

Learning objective

Use the relationship between multiplication and division to solve problems

Basic questions

1 Work these out mentally. Write the answers.

(a) $4 \times 6 =$　　(b) $7 \times 8 =$　　(c) $5 \times 9 =$　　(d) $10 \times 10 =$

　　$24 \div 4 =$　　　　$56 \div 7 =$　　　　$45 \div 9 =$　　　　$100 \div 10 =$

　　$24 \div 6 =$　　　　$56 \div 8 =$　　　　$45 \div 5 =$　　　　$0 \times 7 =$

2 Find the greatest number that will fill in each bracket.

(　　) $\times 5 < 42$　　　　(　　) $\times 6 < 37$　　　　(　　) $\times 8 < 80$

$7 \times$ (　　) < 56　　　　$48 > 9 \times$ (　　)　　　　$58 > 6 \times$ (　　)

3 Draw lines to match the conditions to the questions. Then write the number sentences and calculate. (Each set consists of one desk and one chair.)

There are 6 rows of desks and chairs in the classroom. There are 7 sets in each row.	How many rows are there?
There are 42 sets of desks and chairs. There are 7 sets in each row.	How many sets are there in each row?
There are 42 sets of desks and chairs. They are put into 6 rows equally.	How many sets of desks and chairs are there?

(a) Number sentence：_____　Answer：There are ____ rows.

(b) Number sentence：_____　Answer：There are ____ sets in each row.

(c) Number sentence：_____　Answer：There are ____ sets of desks and chairs.

4 Application problems.

(a) There are 6 giraffes in the zoo. There are 6 times as many deer as the giraffes. How many deer are there?

Answer: _____

(b) 10 boys participated in a school activity of making paper cranes. Each of them made 4 paper cranes. A group of girls made 32 paper cranes in total. Who have made more, the boys or the girls?

Answer: _____

(c) A taxi can seat 4 passengers. There are 27 passengers. At least how many taxis are needed to carry all the passengers?

Answer: _____

(d) The month of July has (   ) weeks and (   ) days. To get the answer, the division sentence is: _____.

Challenge and extension questions

5 There are fewer than 30 cupcakes in a box. If they are given to 4 or 5 children equally, there will be 1 cupcake left over. How many cupcakes are there?

Answer: _____

6 The cost of 1 = the cost of 8 . The cost of 4 pairs of =

the cost of 8 . The cost of 2 = the cost of (   ) .

6.4 Mathematics plaza — dots and patterns

Learning objective

Explore patterns of odd and even numbers

Basic questions

1 Look at the dot diagrams and fill in the brackets with an even number or odd number. (Recall even numbers 0, 2, 4, ⋯ and odd numbers 1, 3, 5, ⋯)

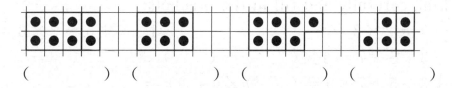

(   ) (   ) (   ) (   )

2 Look at the dot diagrams and write the number sentences.

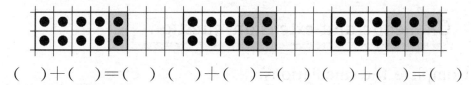

( )+( )=( )　( )+( )=( )　( )+( )=( )

3 Find patterns and then fill in the brackets.

(a) 1, 3, 5, 7, 9, (   ), (   ), (   )

(b) 2, 4, 6, 8, 10, (   ), (   ), (   )

(c) 30, 28, 26, 24, 22, (   ), (   ), (   )

(d) 2, 5, 4, 7, 6, 9, 8, 11, (   ), (   ), (   ), (   )

4 Look at the diagram and fill in the spaces.

○○○　○○○　○○○　○○○　○○○　○

Number sentence: 16÷3=_____ (groups) with a remainder of _____ (circle)

Number sentence: $16 \div 5 =$ _____ (circles) with a remainder of _____ (circle)

⑤ Write the numbers.

(a) 5 odd numbers: (　　　　　)

(b) 5 even numbers: (　　　　　)

(c) All two-digit odd numbers with a 3 in the tens place: (　　　　　).

(d) All two-digit even numbers with a 6 in the tens place: (　　　　　).

(e) 4 two-digit even numbers after 19: (　　　　　).

6　Think carefully and fill in the brackets.

$1 + 3 = 2 \times 2 = ($ 　　 $)$　　　　$1 + 3 + 5 = 3 \times 3 = ($ 　　 $)$

$1 + 3 + 5 + 7 = 4 \times ($ 　 $) = ($ 　 $)$

$1 + 3 + 5 + 7 + 9 = ($ 　 $) \times ($ 　 $) = ($ 　 $)$

$1 + 3 + 5 + 7 + ($ 　 $) + ($ 　 $) = ($ 　 $) \times ($ 　 $) = ($ 　 $)$

Challenge and extension question

❼ Complete the calculations.

$8 + 1 =$ 　　　　　$8 + 2 =$ 　　　　　$9 + 1 =$

$8 + 3 =$ 　　　　　$8 + 4 =$ 　　　　　$9 + 3 =$

$8 + 5 =$ 　　　　　$8 + 6 =$ 　　　　　$9 + 5 =$

$8 + 7 =$ 　　　　　$8 + 8 =$ 　　　　　$9 + 7 =$

Think carefully and fill in the brackets.

even number + odd number = (　　　　　)

even number + even number = (　　　　　)

odd number + odd number = (　　　　　)

6.5 Mathematics plaza — magic square[①]

 Learning objective

Explore patterns on magic squares

 Basic questions

① Calculate and fill in the boxes. Two have been filled in for you.

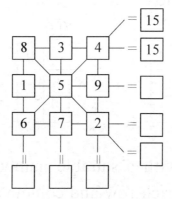

2 Which of these is a magic square? Put a √ for yes and a × for no in the brackets.

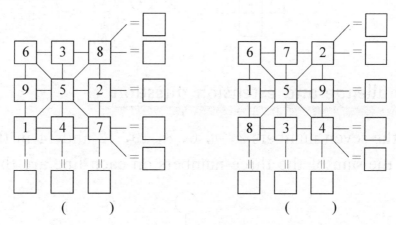

(   )   (   )

---

① In a magic square, each number is used once and all the numbers in every row, column, and diagonal add up to the same number.

3 Fill in each box with a number so that the sum of the three numbers on each line is 15.

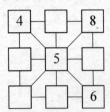
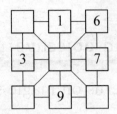

4 Fill in the cells with different numbers so that all the 3 numbers in each row, each column and each diagonal line add up to the number in the circle.

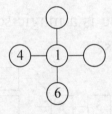

5 Fill in each cell with a suitable number so that the sum of the three numbers in each row and column is 10.

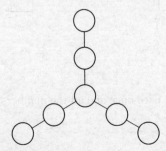

Challenge and extension question

6 Fill the seven numbers 2, 4, 6, 8, 10, 12 and 14 in the circles so that the sum of the three numbers on each line are the same.

6.6 Numbers to 1000 and beyond

 Learning objective

Recognise and use place value of 3-digit and 4-digit numbers

 Basic questions

1. Work these out mentally. Write the answers.

    $57 - 33 + 45 =$ $1 \times 6 \times 6 =$ $64 \div 8 - 0 =$

    $23 + 82 + 92 =$ $6 \times 6 \times 0 =$ $50 \div 5 + 72 =$

2. Complete the place value chart.

......	( ) place	( ) place	( ) place	(tens) place	(ones) place

3. Complete the number pattern.

    1000, 2000, (   ), 4000, (   ), 6000, (   ), 8000, (   ),
    10 000, (   ), 12 000

4. Write the digits of each number in the place value chart. The first one has been done for you.

    4208

Ten thousands	Thousands	Hundreds	Tens	Ones
0	4	2	0	8

    9990

Ten thousands	Thousands	Hundreds	Tens	Ones

    10 008

Ten thousands	Thousands	Hundreds	Tens	Ones

    2006

Ten thousands	Thousands	Hundreds	Tens	Ones

5 Write the numbers represented in each place value chart.

Ten thousands	Thousands	Hundreds	Tens	Ones
	● ●	● ●		● ●

Written in words:_____
Written in numerals: _____

Ten thousands	Thousands	Hundreds	Tens	Ones
●				

Written in words:_____
Written in numerals: _____

Ten thousands	Thousands	Hundreds	Tens	Ones
	● ● ● ● ●	● ●	● ● ●	

Written in words: _____
Written in numerals: _____

Ten thousands	Thousands	Hundreds	Tens	Ones
	● ● ● ●		● ● ● ● ●	● ● ●

Written in words: _____
Written in numerals: _____

6 Fill in the brackets.

(a) 10 ones make (   ), 10 tens make (   ), 10 hundreds make (   ) and 10 thousands make (   ).

(b) Counting from the right, the first digit of a number is its (   ) place. The third digit is its (   ) place. The fifth digit is its (   ) place.

(c) A number consisting of 7 thousands, 5 hundreds, 2 tens and 3 ones is (   ).

(d) There are (   ) thousands or (   ) hundreds in 6000. There are (   ) tens in 170.

(e) Three consecutive numbers after 9998 are (   ), (   ) and (   ).

Challenge and extension question

7 Complete the number patterns.

(a) 5078, 5079, (   ), (   ), 5082

(b) 2323, 3434, 4545, (   ), (   ), 7878

(c) 10 000, 9990, 9980, (   ), (   ), (   )

6.7 Read, write and compare numbers to 1000 and beyond

 Learning objective

Read, write and compare numbers beyond 1000

 Basic questions

1. Work these out mentally. Write the answers.

$70 - 3 + 13 =$ $53 - 37 - 4 =$ $6 \times 8 + 3 =$

$47 - 11 - 21 =$ $6 \times 4 + 61 =$ $40 \div 4 - 5 =$

$90 \div 9 \times 5 =$ $23 + 28 + 92 =$ $4 \times 8 + 6 =$

2. Read and write the numbers in words and numerals to complete the table.

Read and write numbers in words	Write in numerals
Six thousand three hundred and forty-eight	
Five thousand and fifty	
Thirteen thousand and four	
	9008
	4415
	19 006

3. Read and write the numbers in words. Then fill in the blanks.

4632 _____   4632 = _____ + _____ + _____ + _____

2547 _____   2547 = _____ + _____ + _____ + _____

6003 _____   6003 = _____ + _____ + _____ + _____

2030 _____   2030 = _____ + _____ + _____ + _____

4 Write the numbers in numerals.

One thousand eight hundred and twelve: _____

Four thousand and fifty: _____

Six thousand five hundred: _____

Five thousand and six: _____

5 Fill in the ◯ with >, < or =.

985 ◯ 895   1000 ◯ 999   7801 ◯ 7081

3877 ◯ 3787   5020 ◯ 2050   3456 ◯ 3546

5420 ◯ 5421   9887 ◯ 9987   4002 ◯ 4200

6 Multiple choice questions.

(a) Four thousand and five hundred is written as (   ).

   A. 450   B. 4500   C. 4050

(b) Three thousand and seventeen is written as (   ).

   A. 307   B. 3007   C. 3017

(c) Nine thousand and three is written as (   ).

   A. 9030   B. 903   C. 9003

7 Use < to put the numbers in order, from the least to the greatest.

(a) 367   209   627   736   _____

(b) 8070   8007   8700   7800   _____

Challenge and extension question

8 Use the five digits 5, 4, 0, 0 and 9 to write the numbers.

(a) The greatest five-digit number: _____

(b) 0 in the ones place (write three such numbers): _____

(c) 0 not in the ones place (write three such numbers): _____

(d) Greater than 90 000 (write three such numbers): _____

97

Unit test 6

1 Work these out mentally. Write the answers.

$6 \times 4 =$ $9 \times 5 =$ $32 \div 7 =$ $30 \div 5 \times 4 =$

$9 \times 7 =$ $66 \div 8 =$ $10 \times 10 =$ $3 \times 8 + 4 \times 8 =$

$36 \div 6 =$ $0 \div 9 =$ $4 \times 9 - 11 =$ $7 \times 9 - 4 \times 9 =$

$\boxed{} \div 10 = 3 \text{ r } 6$ $19 \div \boxed{} = 3 \text{ r } 1$

2 Find the greatest number that will fill in each bracket.

$7 \times ($ $) < 45$ $31 > 6 \times ($ $)$

$($ $) \times 8 < 40$ $20 > ($ $) \times 9$

3 Fill in the ○ with $+$, $-$, $\times$ or $\div$.

$5 \bigcirc 6 = 11$ $30 \bigcirc 0 = 0$ $9 \bigcirc 3 = 3$

$10 \bigcirc 3 = 30$ $18 \bigcirc 18 = 0$ $30 \bigcirc 5 = 6$

4 Fill in the ○ with $>$, $<$ or $=$.

$2 \times 9 \bigcirc 3 \times 6$ $9 \times 9 \bigcirc 9 + 9$ $4 + 26 \bigcirc 66 - 30$

5 Fill in the brackets.

$2 \times 8 + 7 \times 8 = ($ $) \times 8 = ($ $)$

$10 \times 6 - 4 \times 6 = ($ $) \times 6 = ($ $)$

$7 \times ($ $) < 8 \times 6$ $42 \div 6 = ($ $) \div 8$ $40 \div 5 > ($ $) \times 3$

6 Complete the diagrams and fill in the brackets.

(a) Identify the patterns and fill in the diamonds with suitable multiplication sentences.

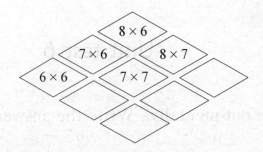

(b) Fill in each cell with a suitable number so that all three numbers in each row, column and diagonal total 15.

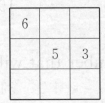

(c) $1+3+5+7+9=($ $)\times5=($ $)$

(d) Given $\triangle\div\bigcirc=5$ r 5, the least possible number $\bigcirc$ is (   ), and then $\triangle$ is (   ).

(e) If $\bigcirc+\bigcirc+\blacktriangle=26$ and $\blacktriangle\times5=40$, then $\bigcirc\times\blacktriangle=($ $)$.

(f) There are 8 cupcakes in each box. Some girls get 24 cupcakes, which is (   ) boxes. Some boys get 4 boxes, which is (   ) cupcakes. There are 22 girls and 18 boys in a class. If each child gets 1 cupcake, then they need (   ) boxes of cupcakes.

7 Fill in the brackets.

(a) Write the numbers in numerals.

Four thousand and five (   )

Six thousand and eight hundred (   )

One thousand and fifty-two (   )

Ten thousand and thirty-nine (   )

(b) 1005 consists of (   ) thousand and (   ) ones. It is written in words as: _____

(c) Put the following numbers in order.

1005, 105, 1050, 501, 5001.

(　　　)<(　　　)<(　　　)<(　　　)<(　　　).

(d) Use the four digits 0, 0, 2 and 4 to write four-digit numbers.

(i) The greatest four-digit number (　　　　).

(ii) The least four-digit number (　　　　).

(iii) Two different numbers with zero in the hundreds places

(　　　), (　　　).

(iv) Four different numbers with zero in ones places

(　　　), (　　　), (　　　), (　　　).

8 Application problems.

(a) 6 cups of water can fill up one kettle. 5 kettles of water can fill up one bucket. How many cups of water can fill up one bucket?

Answer: _____

(b) There are 8 footballs and 32 basketballs in a storage room. How many times as many basketballs are there as footballs?

Answer: _____

(c) Mr Smith and 26 children go rowing. If one boat can seat 6 people, at least how many boats do they need?

Answer: _____

(d) James wanted to buy some yogurts with 17 pounds. Each cup of yogurt costs £2. Did he have enough money to buy 9 cups?

Answer: _____

(e) Some boys get 6 plates of apples. Each plate has 5 apples. Some girls get 32 apples. Who got more apples, the boys or the girls?

Answer: _____

(f) The statistics table shows the number of children in two Year 3 classes in a school participating in different sports clubs.

Sports clubs	badminton	softball	swimming	gymnastics
Number of children	6	12	18	12

(i) Complete a bar chart based on the data in the table above. (Remember to indicate the number of children that 1 unit in your bar chart stands for.)

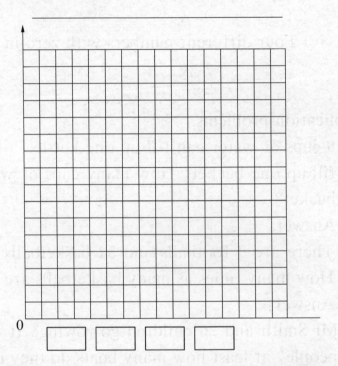

In the graph, 1 unit of the number of children stands for (　　) children.

(ii) There are (　　) fewer children joining the badminton club than the gymnastics club.

(iii) Two clubs are equally popular in terms of the participants. They are the (　　　　) club and the (　　　　) club.

(iv) The most popular club is the (　　　　) club. It has (　　　) times as many participants as the least popular club, which is the (　　) club.

(v) There are (　　) children in total in the two classes who participated in the four sports clubs.

Chapter 7   Addition and subtraction with three-digit numbers

7.1   Addition and subtraction of whole hundreds and tens (1)

 Learning objective

Add and subtract multiples of 10 and 100

 Basic questions

1 Fill in the brackets.

(a) $300 + 200$ means (   ) hundreds plus (   ) hundreds, which makes (   ) hundreds.

(b) $400 + 500$ means (   ) hundreds plus (   ) hundreds, which makes (   ) hundreds.

(c) $900 - 300$ means (   ) hundreds minus (   ) hundreds, which makes (   ) hundreds.

(d) $600 - 400$ means (   ) hundreds minus (   ) hundreds, which makes (   ) hundreds.

2 Work these out mentally. Write the answers.

$500 + 200 =$ $900 - 300 =$ $400 - 100 =$ $200 + 400 =$

$300 + 600 =$ $300 + 200 =$ $400 - 300 =$ $500 - 100 =$

3 Fill in the brackets.

(a) $450 + 20$ means (   ) tens plus (   ) tens, which makes (   ) tens.

(b) $450 - 20$ means (   ) tens minus (   ) tens, which makes (   ) tens.

(c) $360+120$ means ( ) tens plus ( ) tens, which makes ( ) tens.

(d) $360-120$ means ( ) tens minus ( ) tens, which makes ( ) tens.

4 Work these out mentally. Write the answers.

$12+7=$ $120+70=$ $45-8=$ $450-80=$

$35+8=$ $350+80=$ $91-5=$ $910-50=$

5 Fill in the ◯ with $>$, $<$ or $=$.

$800+300$ ◯ $300+800$ $460-40$ ◯ $460+40$

$540+70$ ◯ $40+570$ $690-90$ ◯ $700-90$

6 Application problems.

(a) A washing machine costs £230. A TV set costs £400. How much cheaper is the washing machine than the TV set?

Answer: _____

(b) There are 530 storybooks and 380 science books in a library. How many storybooks and science books are there in total?

Answer: _____

(c) John's father bought him a bike for £380. He paid the shop assistant £400. How much change should he have received?

Answer: _____

(d) There are 340 peach trees in an orchard, which is 270 fewer than apple trees. How many apple trees are there?

Answer: _____

Challenge and extension question

7 Which is greater, ◯ or ▢ ? How much greater is it?

$$◯+150=▢-150$$

7.2 Addition and subtraction of whole hundreds and tens (2)

 Learning objective

Add and subtract multiples of 10 and 100

 Basic questions

1 Work these out mentally. Write the answers.

$870 - 700 =$	$500 + 320 =$	$760 - 560 =$
$900 - 190 =$	$730 + 150 =$	$670 + 300 =$
$370 - 150 =$	$640 + 90 =$	$130 + 370 =$
$360 - 190 =$	$480 - 250 =$	$1000 - 650 =$

2 Complete the table.

(a)

Addend	280	210	330	140	240	390	190
Addend	230	160	150	360	410	220	810
Sum							

(b)

Minuend	160	240	430	650	710	480	610
Subtrahend	80	90	210	360	450	290	450
Difference							

3 Write the sum and the difference of the two numbers on each card.

600		250		460		720
200		80		170		280

Sum: (　) 　　 Sum: (　) 　　 Sum: (　) 　　 Sum: (　)

Difference: (　) Difference: (　) Difference: (　) Difference: (　)

4 Calculate and then fill in each box with your answer.

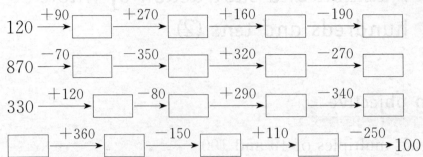

5 Application problems.

(a) Mary and Joan took part in a 800-metre run. When Mary was 200 metres away from the finish line, Joan was 250 metres away. How many metres had each of them run? Who had run faster up to that point in time?

Answer: _____

(b) A school bought 250 apples and gave 90 of them to Year 1 and 110 to Year 2. How many apples were left?

Answer: _____

(c) Tom collected 150 stamps last year. He has collected 280 stamps this year, but he still has 130 stamps fewer than John. How many stamps has John collected?

Answer: _____

(d) A small-sized cinema hall has 30 seats. It has 80 seats fewer than a medium-sized cinema hall. A grand-sized cinema hall has 160 seats more than the medium-sized cinema hall. How many seats does the grand-sized cinema hall have?

Answer: _____

Challenge and extension question

6 Look at the diagram. Fill in each circle with 100, 200, 300, 400, 500 or 600 so that the sum of the four numbers in the corners of each square is 1200.

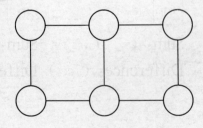

7.3 Adding and subtracting three-digit numbers and ones (1)

 Learning objective

Add and subtract ones from three-digit numbers

 Basic questions

1. Calculate with reasoning.

   $23 + 2 =$ $46 - 8 =$ $52 - 5 =$ $26 + 8 =$

   $323 + 2 =$ $246 - 8 =$ $552 - 5 =$ $426 + 8 =$

2. Work these out mentally. Write the answers.

   $326 + 8 =$ $113 - 5 =$ $312 + 8 =$ $119 - 8 =$

   $223 - 4 =$ $233 + 8 =$ $450 - 6 =$ $592 + 8 =$

3. Complete these addition and subtraction calculations using the number lines.

   (a) +2   +4

   298 ☐ ☐

   $298 + 6 =$

   (b)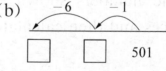

   ☐ ☐ 501

   $501 - 7 =$

   (c) +4   +3

   496 ☐ ☐

   $496 + 7 =$

   (d)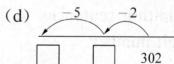

   ☐ ☐ 302

   $302 - 7 =$

4 Complete the tables.

+6

395	
597	

+8

793	
899	

−6

201	
704	

−8

603	
505	

5 Work these out mentally. Write the answers.

$289 + 6 =$ $203 - 5 =$ $495 + 6 =$ $910 - 7 =$

$320 - 4 =$ $698 + 4 =$ $790 - 6 =$ $589 + 2 =$

$503 - 4 =$ $763 + 8 =$ $494 + 6 =$ $388 + 3 =$

6 Calculate and then fill in each box with your answer.

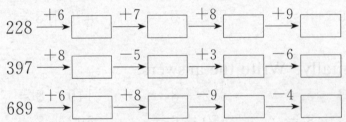

$228 \xrightarrow{+6} \Box \xrightarrow{+7} \Box \xrightarrow{+8} \Box \xrightarrow{+9} \Box$

$397 \xrightarrow{+8} \Box \xrightarrow{-5} \Box \xrightarrow{+3} \Box \xrightarrow{-6} \Box$

$689 \xrightarrow{+6} \Box \xrightarrow{+8} \Box \xrightarrow{-9} \Box \xrightarrow{-4} \Box$

Challenge and extension question

7 Use the numbers shown on the cards below to form number sentences and then calculate.

| 5 | 3 | 7 | 9 | 0 |

(a) Addition sentences to add a three-digit number and a one-digit number.

_____   _____   _____

_____   _____   _____

(b) Subtraction sentences to subtract a one-digit number from a three-digit number.

_____   _____   _____

_____   _____   _____

7.4 Adding and subtracting three-digit numbers and ones (2)

 Learning objective

Add and subtract ones from three-digit numbers

 Basic questions

1 Work these out mentally. Write the answers.

$325 + 8 =$ $590 - 9 =$ $708 + 9 =$ $377 - 8 =$

$278 - 6 =$ $498 + 6 =$ $300 - 3 =$ $799 + 2 =$

$702 - 4 =$ $375 + 5 =$ $256 + 6 =$ $173 + 7 =$

2 Fill in the spaces with suitable numbers.

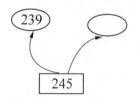   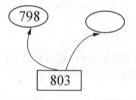   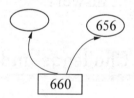

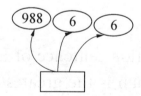   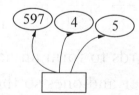   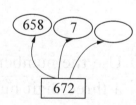

3 Draw lines to match the calculations with the same answers.

627 + 5	702	702 − 7
689 + 6	632	710 − 8
697 + 5	695	641 − 9

4 Application problems.

(a) During an environment protection campaign, some Year 2 children collected 203 used batteries, which was 9 fewer than the number of batteries collected by Year 3. How many batteries did the Year 3 children collect?

Answer: _____

(b) Tom is 132 cm tall. He is 5 cm taller than Mary. What is the height of Mary?

Answer: _____

(c) An appliance shop had 256 TV sets and then sold 8 sets in the morning and 7 sets in the afternoon. How many TV sets did the shop still have?

Answer: _____

(d) Max, Mary and Jo were playing rope skipping. Max did 142 skips. He did 6 skips fewer than Jo and Mary did 8 skips fewer than Jo. How many skips did Mary do?

Answer: _____

Challenge and extension question

5 Look at the number cards and answer the questions.

4 8 9 2

(a) Use the number cards to form an addition sentence of adding a three-digit number and ones so the sum is the greatest.

_____

(b) Use the number cards to form a subtraction sentence of subtracting a one-digit number from a three-digit number so the difference is the least.

_____

7.5 Addition with three-digit numbers (1)

Learning objective

Use partitioning to add three-digit numbers

Basic questions

1 Calculate with reasoning.

(a) Tom's method.

$322 + 216 =$ _____

> Hundreds+Hundreds: $300 + 200 =$ ____
> Tens+Tens: $20 + 10 =$ ____
> Ones+Ones: $2 + 6 =$ ____
> ____ + ____ + ____ = ____

(b) Mary's method.

$132 + 454 =$ _____

> Ones+Ones: ____ + ____ = ____
> Tens+Tens: ____ + ____ = ____
> Hundreds+Hundreds: ____ + ____ = ____
> ____ + ____ + ____ = ____

(c) Joan's method.

$124 + 259$	$379 + 146$
$= 124 + 200 + 50 + 9$	$= 379 +$ ____ $+$ ____ $+$ ____
$=$ ____ $+$ ____ $+$ ____	$=$ ____ $+$ ____ $+$ ____
$=$ ____ $+$ ____	$=$ ____ $+$ ____
$=$ ____	$=$ ____

(d) John's method.

$$430+352$$
$$=430+2+50+300$$
$$=\underline{\quad}+\underline{\quad}+\underline{\quad}$$
$$=\underline{\quad}+\underline{\quad}$$
$$=\underline{\quad}$$

$$182+219$$
$$=182+\underline{\quad}+\underline{\quad}+\underline{\quad}$$
$$=\underline{\quad}+\underline{\quad}+\underline{\quad}$$
$$=\underline{\quad}+\underline{\quad}$$
$$=\underline{\quad}$$

2 Use your preferred method to calculate. Show your working.

$$536+121 \qquad 428+236 \qquad 650+328 \qquad 418+365$$

3 First use the six number cards to form addition sentences of adding 2 three-digit numbers. Then work them out with your preferred method.

| 6 | 0 | 7 | 3 | 5 | 2 |

(a) _____ (b) _____ (c) _____

4 Write number sentences and then calculate.

(a) One addend is 239 and the other is 384. What is the sum?

Number sentence: _____

(b) What number is 168 more than 574?

Number sentence: _____

Challenge and extension question

5 Fill in the brackets.

(a) The sum of the least three-digit number and the least three-digit number is a (   )-digit number.

(b) The sum of the greatest three-digit number and the greatest three-digit number is a (   )-digit number.

(c) The sum of 2 three-digit numbers can be a (   )-digit number or a (   )-digit number.

7.6 Addition with three-digit numbers (2)

Learning objective

Use the column method to add three-digit numbers

Basic questions

1. Use the column method to calculate.

(a) $450+234=$

```
    4  5  0
  + 2  3  4
```

(b) $308+126=$

```
    3  0  8
  + 1  2  6
```

(c) $703+224=$

```
    7  0  3
  + 2  2  4
```

(d) $372+143=$ (e) $346+251=$ (f) $597+188=$

2. Are these calculations correct? Put a $\sqrt{}$ for yes and a $\times$ for no in each bracket and then make corrections.

(a)
```
    5  8  1
  + 3  3
  ─────────
    9  1  1
```
(   )

(b)
```
    3  7  8
  + 1  2  6
  ─────────
    4  9  4
```
(   )

(c)
```
    3  5  4
  + 1  2  8
  ─────────
    4  8  2
```
(   )

Correction:

3 Complete the table.

Addend	327	204	534	178	257	689
Addend	150	328	265	433	465	311
Sum						

4 Fill in the boxes.

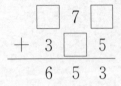

```
  □ 7 □            4 6 □            3 □ 6
+ 3 □ 5          + □ □ 2          + □ 2 □
─────────        ─────────        ─────────
  6 5 3            8 0 0            7 1 8
```

5 Application problems.

(a) An electrician cut off 312 metres from an electric wire. He then cut off another 268 metres. How many metres did he cut off in total?

Answer: _____

(b) Ollie was reading a book. He read 162 pages in the first week, which were 135 fewer pages than the second week. How many pages did he read in the second week?

Answer: _____

(c) At an online store, a used laptop computer is priced at £138. A new laptop is priced at £162 more. How much is the price of the new laptop?

Answer: _____

Challenge and extension question

6 When John did an addition sentence, by mistake he took the digit 3 in the hundreds place as 2 and the digit 7 in the ones place as 1. The sum he obtained was 675. What is the correct sum?

7.7 Subtraction with three-digit numbers (1)

 Learning objective

Use partitioning to subtract three-digit numbers

 Basic questions

① Calculate with reasoning.

(a) Tom's method.

$467 - 253 = $ _____

> Hundreds—Hundreds: $400 - 200 = $ ____
> Tens—Tens: $60 - 50 = $ ____
> Ones—Ones: $7 - 3 = $ ____
> ____ + ____ + ____ = ____

(b) Mary's method.

$856 - 543 = $ _____

> Subtract hundreds first: $856 - 500 = $ ____
> Then subtract tens: ____ − ____ = ____
> Finally subtract ones: ____ − ____ = ____

(c) Joan's method.

$356 - 185$ $637 - 249$
$= 356 - 100 - 80 - 5$ $= 637 - $ ____ − ____ − ____
$= $ ____ − ____ − ____ $= $ ____ − ____ − ____
$= $ ____ − ____ $= $ ____ − ____
$= $ ____ $= $ ____

Addition and subtraction with three-digit numbers

(d) John's method.

$606-347$

$=606-7-40-300$

$=\underline{\quad}-\underline{\quad}-\underline{\quad}$

$=\underline{\quad}-\underline{\quad}$

$=\underline{\quad}$

$534-397$

$=534-\underline{\quad}-\underline{\quad}-\underline{\quad}$

$=\underline{\quad}-\underline{\quad}-\underline{\quad}$

$=\underline{\quad}-\underline{\quad}$

$=\underline{\quad}$

2 Use your preferred method to calculate. Show your working.

$788-323$ $\qquad$ $900-167$ $\qquad$ $459-366$ $\qquad$ $558-263$

3 Use the six number cards below to form subtraction sentences of subtracting a three-digit number from another three-digit number. Then calculate using your preferred method.

| 8 | 1 | 7 | 9 | 4 | 0 |

(a) _____ (b) _____ (c) _____

4 Write number sentences and calculate.

(a) The minuend is 429 and the subtrahend is 290. What is the difference?

Answer: _____

(b) What number is 348 less than 695?

Answer: _____

Challenge and extension question

5 The mass of 1 pack of salt and 1 pack of sugar in total is 470 grams. The mass of 2 packs of salt and 1 pack of sugar is 630 grams. What is the mass of 1 pack of salt? What is the mass of 1 pack of sugar?

7.8 Subtraction with three-digit numbers (2)

Learning objective

Use the column method to subtract three-digit numbers

Basic questions

1 Use the columnar method to calculate.

(a) $187-31=$

```
   1 8 7
 -   3 1
 ───────
```

(b) $129-88=$

```
   1 2 9
 -   8 8
 ───────
```

(c) $151-75=$

```
   1 5 1
 -   7 5
 ───────
```

(d) $433-265=$

```
   4 3 3
 - 2 6 5
 ───────
```

(e) $800-468=$

```
   8 0 0
 - 4 6 8
 ───────
```

(f) $105-76=$

```
   1 0 5
 -   7 6
 ───────
```

2 Are these calculations correct? Put a √ for yes and a ✕ for no in each bracket and then make corrections.

(a)
```
   6 4 3
 - 3 0 7
 ───────
   3 4 6
  (   )
```

(b)
```
   4 1 3
 - 3 3 1
 ───────
   1 4 2
  (   )
```

(c)
```
   1 0 5
 -   3 9
 ───────
   7 6
  (   )
```

Correction:

3 Complete the table.

Minuend	737	562	656	770	312	707
Subtrahend	133	266	475	634	134	668
Difference						

4 Fill in the boxes.

```
  □ 5 □              4 6 □              6 □ 3
-  3 □ 5           - □ □ 6            - □ 2 □
  2 5 3              2 0 6              4 8
```

5 Application problems.

an airplane flies at
769 km per hour

a high-speed train runs at
372 km per hour

a car runs at
112 km per hour

(a) How many more kilometres does the airplane fly than the high-speed train per hour?

Answer：_____

(b) How many fewer kilometres does the car run than the high-speed train per hour?

Answer：_____

(c) Using "how many more" or "how many fewer", write your own question based on the pictures above.

_____

 Challenge and extension question

6 Fill in the boxes and complete the sentences.

```
  5 □ 2
- 4 3 9
```

(a) If the difference is a three-digit number, the least possible number in the □ is (   ).

(b) If the difference is a two-digit number, the greatest possible number in the □ is (   ).

7.9 Estimating addition and subtraction with three-digit numbers (1)

 Learning objective

Estimate and calculate the answers to addition and subtraction problems

 Basic questions

1 Work these out mentally. Write the answers.

$320 + 80 =$ $310 - 90 =$ $580 + 100 =$ $102 - 29 =$

$720 - 60 =$ $490 + 60 =$ $670 - 600 =$ $390 + 200 =$

2 Complete the table. The first one has been done for you.

	232	527	659	707	348	499
The nearest whole ten	230					
The nearest whole hundred	200					

3 Estimate to the nearest ten first and then calculate.

$212 + 168$ $438 + 321$ $192 + 306$

Estimate:_____   Estimate:_____   Estimate:_____

Calculate:_____   Calculate:_____   Calculate:_____

$626 + 322$ $674 - 418$ $813 - 479$

Estimate:_____   Estimate:_____   Estimate:_____

Calculate:_____   Calculate:_____   Calculate:_____

4 Estimate to the nearest hundred first and then calculate.

$388 + 217$ $657 + 129$ $290 + 426$

Estimate:_____   Estimate:_____   Estimate:_____

Calculate:_____   Calculate:_____   Calculate:_____

587＋349   477－286   529－380

Estimate: _____   Estimate: _____   Estimate: _____

Calculate: _____   Calculate: _____   Calculate: _____

5 Application problems.

(a) A school organises 228 Year 4 and 198 Year 5 children to go swimming at a local pool. There cannot be more than 450 children in the swimming pool at the same time. Estimate whether all these children can swim at the same time.

Answer: _____

(b) There are 287 peach trees and 343 pear trees in an orchard. Estimate the total number of peach trees and pear trees, and the difference between the two types of trees.

Number of peach and pear trees: _____

Difference: _____

(c) Joan went to a bookstore with £200. She bought two dictionaries for £79 and a set of fairy tale books for £114.

(i) Estimate whether Joan had enough money for the dictionaries and books she bought.

Answer: _____

(ii) If she had enough money, how much change should she get? If she did not have enough, how much was she short of?

Answer: _____

Challenge and extension question

6 A number consists of three digits: 6, 4 and 2.

(a) Adding the number to 350, the result is between 600 and 700. This number is (   ).

(b) Subtracting 350 from the number, the result is between 100 and 200. This number is (   ).

7.10 Estimating addition and subtraction with three-digit numbers (2)

 Learning objective

Estimate and calculate the answers to addition and subtraction problems

 Basic questions

1 Work these out mentally. Write the answers.

$450 + 160 =$ $660 - 450 =$ $370 + 270 =$ $610 - 270 =$

$480 - 330 =$ $530 + 160 =$ $360 + 550 =$ $1000 - 430 =$

2 Estimate first. Then calculate.

$$431 + 278 \qquad\qquad\qquad 516 + 483$$

To the nearest ten: _____   To the nearest ten: _____

To the nearest hundred: _____   To the nearest hundred: _____

Calculate: _____   Calculate: _____

$$878 - 356 \qquad\qquad\qquad 623 - 399$$

To the nearest ten: _____   To the nearest ten: _____

To the nearest hundred: _____   To the nearest hundred: _____

Calculate: _____   Calculate: _____

3 Calculate with reasoning. (Start with the easiest calculation. Think carefully about which one to start with.)

$97 + 238 =$ $456 + 98 =$ $200 - 130 =$ $550 - 97 =$

$98 + 238 =$ $456 + 99 =$ $199 - 130 =$ $550 - 98 =$

$99 + 238 =$ $456 + 100 =$ $198 - 230 =$ $550 - 99 =$

$100 + 238 =$ $456 + 101 =$ $197 - 230 =$ $550 - 100 =$

4 Fill in each bracket with the letter of the correct answer.

A. $213+176$	B. $323+268$	C. $334+178$	D. $352+278$
E. $138+363$	F. $233+171$	G. $268+326$	H. $382+156$

(a) Estimating to the nearest hundred, the number sentence(s) with the result of 400 is/are (　　), that with 500 is/are (　　) and that with 600 is/are (　　).

(b) Estimating to the nearest ten, the number sentence(s) with the result of 400 is/are (　　), that with 500 is/are (　　) and that with 600 is/are (　　).

(c) Now calculate.

$213+176=$　　$323+268=$　　$334+178=$　　$352+278=$

$138+363=$　　$233+171=$　　$268+326=$　　$382+156=$

5 Use the information in the table to estimate the answers.

Name of building in London	Broadgate Tower	One Churchill Place	Canary Wharf Tower	The Shard
Height (metres)	178	156	244	310

(a) About how many metres higher is The Shard than Broadgate Tower?

Answer: _____

(b) About how many metres shorter is One Churchill Place than Canary Wharf Tower?

Answer: _____

(c) Write two more estimation questions of your own, then work out the answers.

_____

Challenge and extension question

6 Choose six of the seven numbers 123, 234, 345, 456, 567, 678 and 789 to fill in the brackets. (Think carefully: how many different ways are there to fill in the brackets?)

(　　)+(　　) =(　　)+(　　)=(　　)+(　　)

Unit test 7

1 Work these out mentally. Write the answers.

$145 + 70 =$ $180 - 18 =$ $570 + 300 =$ $400 - 180 =$

$390 - 66 =$ $243 + 52 =$ $610 - 280 =$ $150 + 68 =$

2 Use the column method to calculate.

(a) $217 + 38 =$ (b) $384 + 138 =$ (c) $157 - 48 =$

(d) $500 - 326 =$ (e) $108 + 39 =$ (f) $101 - 66 =$

3 Estimate to the nearest hundred first and then calculate.

(a) Estimate to the nearest hundred first and then calculate.

$276 + 117$ $381 + 207$

Estimate:_____   Estimate:_____

Calculate: _____   Calculate: _____

$512 - 296$ $389 - 209$

Estimate:_____   Estimate:_____

Calculate: _____   Calculate: _____

(b) Estimate to the nearest ten first and then calculate.

$332 + 176$ $168 + 223$

Estimate:_____   Estimate:_____

Calculate: _____   Calculate: _____

389—277

Estimate: _____

Calculate: _____

501—137

Estimate: _____

Calculate: _____

4 Fill in the boxes.

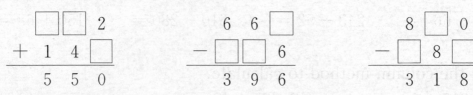

5 Write the number sentences and calculate.

(a) The sum of two addends is 560. One addend is 388. What is the other addend?

Number sentence: _____

(b) What number is 39 less than 105?

Number sentence: _____

(c) The subtrahend is 288 and the difference is 109. What is the minuend?

Number sentence: _____

6 A primary school has 337 boys and 368 girls. How many children are there altogether?

7 A large refrigerator costs £678. John's mother paid the shop assistant £700. How much change should she receive?

8 In a charity activity, the children in Year 1 donated 187 books. The Year 2 children donated 226 books. How many more books did Year 2 donate than Year 1?

9 Tom has collected 295 British postage stamps and 127 other countries' postage stamps. How many stamps has Tom collected in total?

Tom collected 250 of these stamps this year and the rest last year. How many stamps did he collect last year?

10 There are 215 tonnes of sand in a construction site. The amount of cement is 36 tonnes fewer than that of sand and 78 tonnes fewer than that of gravel. How many tonnes of cement are there in the construction site?

What is the amount of gravel?

Chapter 8   Simple fractions and their addition and subtraction

8.1   Unit fractions and tenths

 Learning objective

Use fractions of amounts and count in tenths

 Basic questions

1 Fill in each bracket with a fraction to represent the shaded part.

(a)   (   )

(b)   (   )

(c)   (   )

(d)   (   )

(e)   (   )

(f)   (   )

In the above fractions, the unit fractions are (   ).

2 Circle the objects in each diagram to indicate the fraction given.

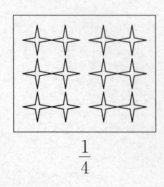

$\dfrac{1}{4}$

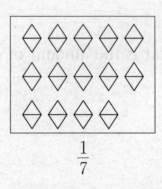

$\dfrac{1}{7}$

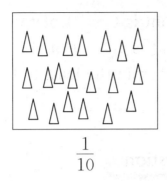

$$\frac{1}{10}$$

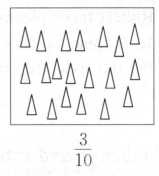

$$\frac{3}{10}$$

3 Fill in the boxes and the brackets with suitable numbers.

(a)

(b)
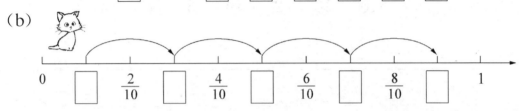

Each unit on the number line is (   ). starts to jump

from (   ). It jumps (   ) units each time and finally

reaches (   ).

(c)
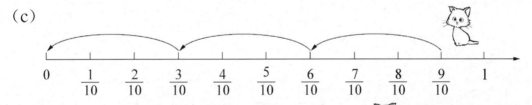

Each unit on the number line is (   ). jumps back from

(   ). It jumps (   ) units each time and finally reaches

(   ).

4 Mum divided a cake into 10 equal pieces for her four children to share. Express the amount of cake each child took as indicated in tenths.

(a) Jim took one piece. The amount is (   ) of the cake.

(b) Amanda took 3 pieces. The amount is (   ) of the cake.

(c) Robert too 2 pieces. The amount is (   ) of the cake.

(d) Kate took 4 pieces. The amount is (   ) of the cake.

(e) Put the above fractions in order from the least to the greatest:

_____

Challenge and extension question

5 Write the unit fractions and tenths in order, from the least to the greatest. (Hint: you may use a number line to help you.)

$$\frac{1}{10}, \quad \frac{9}{10}, \quad \frac{1}{2}, \quad \frac{7}{10}, \quad \frac{1}{5}, \quad \frac{3}{10}, \quad \frac{1}{4}$$

_____

8.2 Non-unit fractions

Learning objective

Use non-unit fractions of amounts

Basic questions

1 Count the items in each picture and fill in the brackets with fractions.

(a)

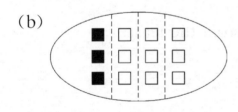

The number of apples is (   ) of the total.

The number of strawberries is (   ) of the total.

The number of apples and bananas is (   ) of the total.

(b)

The number of black squares is (   ) of the total.

The number of white squares is (   ) of the total.

(c) Which fractions you filled in above are unit fractions?

(   )

Which fractions you filled in above are non-unit fractions?

(   )

2 Fill in each bracket with a fraction to represent the shaded part.

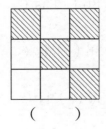

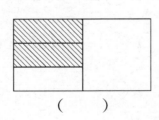

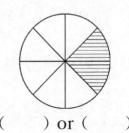

(   )   (   )   (   ) or (   )

128

3 Does each fraction below represent the shaded part of the whole correctly? Put a √ for yes and a × for no in each bracket.

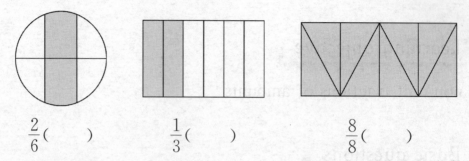

$\frac{2}{6}$ (   ) $\frac{1}{3}$ (   ) $\frac{8}{8}$ (   )

4 Fill in the brackets.

(a) A 1-metre long ribbon is cut into 7 pieces equally. Each piece is (   ) metres long. 4 pieces are (   ) metres long.

(b) $\frac{2}{15}$ of 15 ▲ is (   ) ▲. $\frac{1}{5}$ of 15 ▲ is (   ) ▲.

$\frac{2}{5}$ of 15 ▲ is (   ) ▲. $\frac{3}{5}$ of 15 ▲ is (   ) ▲.

5 Write numbers in order, starting from the least.

(a) $\frac{1}{7}$, $\frac{5}{7}$, $\frac{6}{7}$, $\frac{4}{7}$ and $\frac{2}{7}$. _____

(b) $\frac{4}{9}$, $\frac{2}{9}$, $\frac{8}{9}$, $\frac{7}{9}$ and 1. _____

 Challenge and extension question

6 Calculate these and fill in the brackets. (Hint: you may draw diagrams to help find the answers.)

(a) $\frac{2}{18}$ of 36 ◯ is (   ) ◯.   (b) $\frac{2}{12}$ of 36 ◯ is (   ) ◯.

(c) $\frac{2}{9}$ of 36 ◯ is (   ) ◯.   (d) $\frac{2}{6}$ of 36 ◯ is (   ) ◯.

(e) $\frac{2}{4}$ of 36 ◯ is (   ) ◯.   (f) $\frac{2}{3}$ of 36 ◯ is (   ) ◯.

8.3   Equivalent fractions

 Learning objective

Recognise and show equivalent fractions

 Basic questions

1 Look at the diagram and fill in the brackets.

(a)

The rectangle is divided into 4 parts equally. Each part is (   )
of the whole. 4 parts are (   ) of the whole. It is (   ).

(b) 6 one-sixths are (   ). It is 1.

2 Look at each picture and fill in the brackets with two different
fractions. (You may discuss the answers with your friends.)

(a)

(   ) or (   )

(b)

(   ) or (   )

(c)

(   ) or (   )

3 Fill in the brackets.

(a) 10 one-tenths of a pound are $\dfrac{(\quad)}{(\quad)}$. It is (   ) pound.

(b) Fill in the brackets with $>$, $<$ or $=$.

$\dfrac{1}{12}$(   )$\dfrac{1}{9}$ $\dfrac{4}{10}$(   )$\dfrac{2}{10}$ $\dfrac{3}{3}$(   )$\dfrac{9}{9}$

(c) 4 one-fourths is $\dfrac{(\quad)}{(\quad)}$. It is (   ).

(d) $\dfrac{1}{4}$ of 8 chocolates is (   ) chocolates.

130

(e) 4 one-sixths are $\dfrac{(\quad)}{(\quad)}$. 5 $\dfrac{(\quad)}{(\quad)}$ are $\dfrac{5}{5}$ and it is (　　).

(f) Mr Lee has 3 cockerels and 5 hens. The number of hens is $\dfrac{(\quad)}{(\quad)}$ of the total number of chickens.

4　Circle equivalent fractions and then draw lines to match them.

$$\dfrac{1}{2} \qquad \dfrac{5}{6} \qquad \dfrac{2}{7} \qquad \dfrac{3}{5} \qquad \dfrac{4}{6} \qquad \dfrac{3}{4}$$

$$\dfrac{4}{14} \qquad \dfrac{2}{3} \qquad \dfrac{6}{10} \qquad \dfrac{3}{6} \qquad \dfrac{10}{12} \qquad \dfrac{9}{12}$$

 ## Challenge and extension questions

5　Fill in each bracket with a fraction to represent the shaded part.

(a) 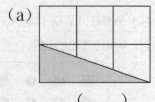　　　(b)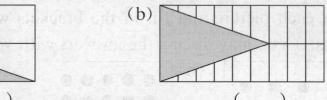

　　(　　)　　　　　　　　　　(　　)

6　Think carefully about how to answer these.

(a) If 48 bottles of coke are divided into 8 parts equally, each part has (　　) bottles of coke. If they are divided into 6 parts equally, each part has (　　) bottles of coke.

(b) If Lily takes away $\dfrac{3}{8}$ of the coke and James takes away $\dfrac{2}{6}$, then (　　) takes more.

(c) If John wants to take $\dfrac{1}{5}$, is it possible? Explain why/why not?

　　Answer：_____

(d) What fraction of coke can John take? Explain why.

　　Answer：_____

8.4 Addition and subtraction of simple fractions

 Learning objective

Add and subtract fractions with the same denominator

 Basic questions

1 Look at the diagrams and add the fractions.

(a) $\dfrac{1}{4} + \dfrac{2}{4} = (\quad)$

(b) $\dfrac{2}{7} + \dfrac{3}{7} = (\quad)$

(c) $\dfrac{3}{8} + \dfrac{5}{8} = (\quad) = (\quad)$

2 Look at the diagrams and complete the subtraction of fractions.

(a) $\dfrac{4}{5} - \dfrac{1}{5} = (\quad)$

(b) $\dfrac{7}{8} - \dfrac{3}{8} = (\quad) = (\quad)$

3 Calculate with addition of fractions.

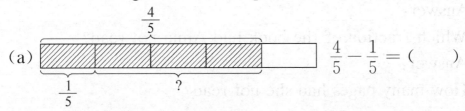

(a) $\dfrac{1}{2} + \dfrac{1}{2} =$ 　　　(b) $\dfrac{2}{7} + \dfrac{4}{7} =$ 　　　(c) $\dfrac{1}{4} + \dfrac{3}{4} =$

(d) $\dfrac{1}{3}+\dfrac{1}{3}=$ (e) $\dfrac{5}{9}+\dfrac{2}{9}=$ (f) $\dfrac{3}{5}+\dfrac{2}{5}=$

4 Calculate with subtraction of fractions.

(a) $\dfrac{5}{8}-\dfrac{3}{8}=$ (b) $1-\dfrac{1}{2}=$ (c) $\dfrac{4}{9}-\dfrac{4}{9}=$

(d) $\dfrac{6}{7}-\dfrac{1}{7}=$ (e) $\dfrac{3}{4}-\dfrac{1}{4}=$ (f) $\dfrac{4}{5}-0=$

5 Anna was reading a book. The book had 24 pages in total. She read 3 pages on the first day, 4 pages on the second day and 5 pages on the third day.

(a) Express the fraction of the book Anna read on each day.

First day: _____ Second day: _____ Third day: _____

(b) What fraction of the book did Anna read on the first two days?

Answer: _____

(c) What fraction of the book had Anna read on the first three days?

Answer: _____

(d) Which fraction of the book had Anna not read?

Answer: _____

How many pages had she not read?

Answer: _____

Challenge and extension question

6 Fill in the brackets.

Joan's grandma bought 12 pears to share. She gave Joan and Joan's brother Tom 3 pears each. She then kept 1 pear to herself and gave the rest to Joan's mother.

(a) Grandma got (   ) of all the pears, Joan got (   ) of all the pears, Tom got (   ) of all the pears, and Joan's mother got (   ) of all the pears. (Fill in with fractions.)

(b) What fraction of all the pears did Joan and her brother get in total? Write the number sentence and calculate the answer.

Number sentence: _____

(c) What fraction of all the pears did Joan, her brother and mother get altogether?

Number sentence: _____

(d) Who got the most? Who got the least? What is the difference? (Write the number sentence and find the difference in fraction.)

Answer: _____ got the most; _____ got the least.

The difference is: _____ = _____ of the total appears. It is (   ) pears.

Unit test 8

1 Fill in the brackets.

(a) If 10 eggs are shared by 10 children equally, one child gets ( ) of all the eggs. Five children get ( ) or ( ) of all the eggs.

(b) $1 = \dfrac{(\quad)}{2} = \dfrac{10}{(\quad)} = \dfrac{(\quad)}{15}$.

(c) 4 ( ) is $\dfrac{4}{6}$. It is read as ( ).

Seven eighths is written as ( ).

(d) $\dfrac{2}{5}$ of the 10 △ are ( ). $\dfrac{1}{3}$ of ( ) ☆ is 4 ☆.

(e) The fewer parts are equally divided from the same whole, the ( ) each part becomes. The ( ) parts are divided equally, the smaller each part becomes.

2 Compare the fractions using the diagrams below. Fill in the ◯ with >, < or =.

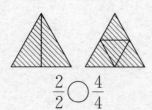

$\dfrac{2}{2}$ ◯ $\dfrac{4}{4}$

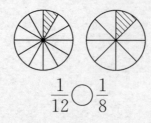

$\dfrac{1}{12}$ ◯ $\dfrac{1}{8}$

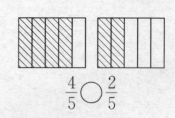

$\dfrac{4}{5}$ ◯ $\dfrac{2}{5}$

3 Draw lines to match the equivalent fractions.

$\dfrac{2}{3}$ $\dfrac{4}{5}$ $\dfrac{7}{8}$ $\dfrac{1}{3}$ $\dfrac{5}{10}$

$\dfrac{3}{9}$ $\dfrac{4}{8}$ $\dfrac{4}{6}$ $\dfrac{8}{10}$ $\dfrac{14}{16}$

4 Write the fractions in order, from the least to the greatest.

(a) $\dfrac{1}{5}$, $\dfrac{1}{12}$, $\dfrac{1}{9}$, $\dfrac{1}{2}$ and 1 _____

(b) $\dfrac{5}{7}$, $\dfrac{4}{7}$, $\dfrac{2}{7}$, $\dfrac{6}{7}$ and 1 _____

5 Work out these calculations.

(a) $\dfrac{1}{4}+\dfrac{1}{4}=$ (b) $\dfrac{7}{9}-\dfrac{2}{9}=$ (c) $\dfrac{3}{10}+\dfrac{7}{10}=$

(d) $\dfrac{2}{3}-\dfrac{1}{3}=$ (e) $\dfrac{1}{11}+\dfrac{8}{11}=$ (f) $\dfrac{1}{5}+\dfrac{4}{5}=$

(g) $\dfrac{7}{10}-\dfrac{3}{10}=$ (h) $\dfrac{1}{5}-\dfrac{1}{5}=$ (i) $1-\dfrac{7}{8}=$

6 Look at the diagram and answer the questions.

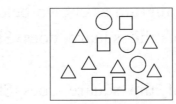

(a) There are (   ) geometric shapes altogether.

(b) Out of the number of all the shapes, the number of ○ takes up $\dfrac{(\quad)}{(\quad)}$, the number of □ takes up $\dfrac{(\quad)}{(\quad)}$, and the number of △ takes up $\dfrac{(\quad)}{(\quad)}$.

(c) What fraction of all the shapes is the number of □ and △ altogether? Write the number sentence and calculate.

Number sentence: _____

(d) What shape takes up the greatest fraction of all the shapes? What shape takes up the least? What is the difference?

Answer: _____ takes up the greatest fraction of all the shapes; _____ takes up the least.

The difference is: _____

7 12 toys were given to two boys and two girls. Amy got 3 toys, Jason got 4 toys, Robert got 2 toys and Ruth got the rest. Use your knowledge of fractions to answer the questions.

(a) What fraction of the toys did Amy get?

Answer: _____

(b) What fraction of the toys did Jason and Robert get altogether?

Answer: _____

(c) Did the boys and girls get the same quantity of toys?

Answer: _____

8 Have you played Tangram? It is a puzzle consisting of seven flat shapes, called tans. The seven shapes can be put together in different ways. You can make thousands of beautiful designs with this simple seven-piece magic puzzle! Let's do some fraction problems using the Tangram as shown below.

(a) What fraction of the square does Shape ① take up?   (   ).

(b) What fraction of the square does Shape ④ take up?   (   ).

(c) What fraction of the square does Shape ⑦ take up?   (   ).

(d) What fraction of the square does Shape ⑤ take up?   (   ).

(e) What fraction of the square does Shape ③ take up?   (   ).

(f) Write a question of your own and give the answer.

_____

_____

Chapter 9 Multiplying and dividing by a one-digit number

9.1 Multiplying by whole tens and hundreds (1)

 Learning objective

Multiply tens and hundreds by one-digit numbers

 Basic questions

1 Calculate with reasoning.

$4 \times 7 =$ $5 \times 3 =$ $6 \times 9 =$

$4 \times 70 =$ $50 \times 3 =$ $60 \times 9 =$

$4 \times 700 =$ $500 \times 3 =$ $6 \times 90 =$

2 Fill in the brackets.

(a) $60 + 60 + 60 + 60 = ($ $)$

    $($ $) \times ($ $) = ($ $)$

    $200 + 200 + 200 + 200 + 200 = ($ $)$

    $($ $) \times ($ $) = ($ $)$

(b) When calculating 6×30 mentally, you can consider it as 6 multiplied by (   ) tens, which is (   ) tens. So the result of 6×30 is (   ).

(c) There are (   ) zeros at the end in the product of 700×9.

3 Fill in the ◯ with $>$, $<$ or $=$.

(a) 9×50 ◯ 90×5 (b) 40×2 ◯ 3×20

(c) 8×200 ◯ 500×6 (d) 300×3 ◯ 5×200

(e) 7×90 ◯ 6×600 (f) 600×4 ◯ 4×600

4 Draw lines to match.

5 × 70   3500

500 × 7   35

5 × 7000   350

5 × 7   35 000

5 Fill in the brackets.

(a) (   ) × 3 = 1200   (b) 700 × (   ) = 1400

(c) 2000 = (   ) × 400   (d) 3200 = 800 × (   )

6 Write each number sentence and calculate.

(a) What is the sum of 40 nines?

Number sentence: _____

(b) What is 3 times 600?

Number sentence: _____

(c) A number is divided by 400, and both its quotient and the remainder are 8. What is the number?

Number sentence: _____

7 A pack of salt weighs 500 grams. How many kilograms is the weight of 8 packs of salt? (Note: 1 kilogram = 1000 grams)

Answer: _____

 Challenge and extension question

8 One plastic box contains 50 pens. 8 plastic boxes can fit into one large case. The price of each pen is £3. How much would 2 large cases of pens cost?

Answer: _____

9.2 Multiplying by whole tens and hundreds (2)

 Learning objective

Multiply by multiples of ten and hundred

 Basic questions

1 Calculate with reasoning.

$3 \times 9 =$ $4 \times 8 =$ $7 \times 6 =$

$3 \times 90 =$ $40 \times 8 =$ $700 \times 6 =$

$3 \times 900 =$ $4 \times 80 =$ $7 \times 600 =$

$30 \times 90 =$ $40 \times 80 =$ $70 \times 60 =$

2 Fill in the brackets.

(a) When calculating 7×500 mentally, you can consider it as 7 multiplied by (   ) hundreds, which is (   ) hundreds. So the result of 7×500 is (   ).

(b) There are (   ) zeros at the end of the product of 500×6.

3 Fill in the ◯ with >, < or =.

(a) 6×50 ◯ 60×5 (b) 400×5 ◯ 40×50

(c) 7×700 ◯ 900×5 (d) 60×30 ◯ 300×6

(e) 7×800 ◯ 50×10 (f) 900×2 ◯ 3×600

4 Draw lines to match.

5×80	4000
500×8	40
50×800	400
5×8	40 000
500×800	400 000

5 Multiple choice questions.

(a) If $\triangle=3$, $\square=600$, $\bigcirc=80$, then $\square-\triangle\times\bigcirc=($ $)$.

    A. 1800   B. 240   C. 360   D. 300

(b) If $36=\bigstar+\bigstar+\bigstar+\bigstar$, then $70\times\bigstar=($ $)$.

    A. 280   B. 630   C. 560   D. 490

6 Application problems.

(a) A farm has 400 hens. The number of chicks is 4 times that of the hens. How many chicks are there? How many chicks and hens are there in total?

Number of chicks: _____

Total number of chicks and hens: _____

(b) A washing machine costs £300. A laptop computer is 5 times as expensive as the washing machine. How much is a laptop computer?

Answer: _____

How much more expensive is a laptop than a washing machine?

Answer: _____

Challenge and extension question

7 Fill in the brackets.

$2000\times 8 = 200\times ($ $) = ($ $)\times 800 = ($ $)\times 4 = 1000\times$
$($ $) = 100\times ($ $) = ($ $)\times 40 = 500\times ($ $)$

9.3 Writing number sentences

Learning objective

Write number sentences for multiplication problems

Basic questions

1 Write each number sentence and calculate.

(a) There are 6 cupcakes in one box. How many cupcakes are there in 11 boxes?

Number sentence:＿＿＿＿＿＿＿＿＿＿＿＿＿＿＿＿

(b) Joan and 3 friends are going on a trip. Everyone needs to pay £30 for the trip. How much do they pay in total?

Number sentence:＿＿＿＿＿＿＿＿＿＿＿＿＿＿＿＿

(c) There are 4 packs of cashew nuts in one box. Each pack costs £12. How much will 3 boxes of cashew nuts cost?

Number sentence:＿＿＿＿＿＿＿＿＿＿＿＿＿＿＿＿

2 Look at the pictures. Draw lines to match each question to the correct number sentence.

| 12 cans per box | 12 cartons per box | 10 kilograms per sack |
| £70 per box | £45 per box | £50 per sack |

(a) How much do 2 boxes of cashew nuts cost? 4×10

(b) How much do 2 boxes of milk cost? 2×12

(c) How many cartons of milk are there in 2 boxes? 2×70

(d) What is the weight of 4 sacks of rice? 2×45

Challenge and extension questions

3 Draw lines to match the calculations with the answers. Then fill in the brackets.

39×8 26×3 92×4

$\boxed{368}$ $\boxed{312}$ $\boxed{276}$ $\boxed{78}$

The number not paired up is (   ). Can you write a number to pair it up?

4 Write a suitable condition, and then write a number sentence and calculate the answer.

A box can be filled up with 8 pieces of chocolate. _____

_____ .

How many boxes can be filled up with?

5 The two whole numbers whose sum is 16 can be 0 and 16, 1 and 15, 2 and 14, 3 and 13, 4 and 12. Among them, the two numbers whose product is the greatest are (   ) and (   ).

9.4 Multiplying a two-digit number by a one-digit number (1)

Learning objective

Multiply two-digit numbers by one-digit numbers

Basic questions

1 Look at the diagram and then complete the multiplication and addition calculations.

```
* * * * * * * * * * * *
* * * * * * * * * * * *
* * * * * * * * * * * *
* * * * * * * * * * * *
* * * * * * * * * * * *
* * * * * * * * * * * *
```

How many * are there altogether?

I use multiplication to find it out. $13 \times 6 = ?$

Split 13 into 10 and 3 first and multiply each by 6. Then add the two products.

First multiply:

( )×( )=( ),   ( )×( )=( );

then add:

( )+( )=( );

therefore:

$13 \times 6 = ($).

2 Work out these calculations.

$7 \times 74 =$ $26 \times 8 =$ $64 \times 9 =$

_____   _____   _____

_____   _____   _____

_____   _____   _____

$2 \times 93 =$ $89 \times 6 =$ $5 \times 54 =$

_____   _____   _____

_____   _____   _____

_____   _____   _____

3 Application problems.

(a) A group of Year 3 children are gathered in a school's sports hall. Each row has 15 children and there are 8 rows. How many children are there altogether?

(b) In a school, 24 children joined the football team. The number of children that joined the choir is twice the number that joined the football team. How many children joined the choir?

Challenge and extension question

4 Fill in the ◯ with $>$ or $<$.

$14 \times 7 ◯ 17 \times 4$ $27 \times 3 ◯ 23 \times 7$

$19 \times 5 ◯ 15 \times 9$ $45 \times 2 ◯ 42 \times 5$

What can you find?

9.5 Multiplying a two-digit number by a one-digit number (2)

Learning objective

Multiply two-digit numbers by one-digit numbers

Basic questions

1 What is the total cost of 3 model sailing boats?

Model sailing boat: £81   Model sailing boat: £81   Model sailing boat: £81

$3 \times 81 =$

Method 1:

```
    8 1
×     3
  □ □ □
```

> Usually, the number with more digits is placed on the top row.

Method 2:

```
      8 1
×       3
        3  ······ □ × □
    2 4 0  ······ □ × □
    2 4 3
```

Answer: The total cost of 3 model sailing boats is _____ pounds.

2 One model car costs £49. How much do two model cars cost?

$49 \times 2 = \boxed{}$ Check the answer: $2 \times 49 = \boxed{}$

$$\begin{array}{r} 4 \;\; 9 \\ \times \qquad 2 \\ \hline \boxed{} \end{array}$$

$2 \times 40 = \boxed{}$

$2 \times 9 = \boxed{}$

$\boxed{} + \boxed{} = \boxed{}$

Do you have another method to check the answer?

3 Use the column method to calculate. Don't forget to check your work with your preferred method.

$4 \times 62 =$ $32 \times 2 =$ $17 \times 5 =$ $7 \times 51 =$

$$\begin{array}{r} \times \\ \hline \end{array} \qquad \begin{array}{r} \times \\ \hline \end{array} \qquad \begin{array}{r} \times \\ \hline \end{array} \qquad \begin{array}{r} \times \\ \hline \end{array}$$

4 Is each of the following calculations correct? Put a $\checkmark$ for yes and a $\times$ for no in the bracket and make your correction in the box.

$$\begin{array}{r} 1 \;\; 4 \\ \times \qquad 4 \\ \hline 4 \;\; 6 \\ (\quad) \end{array} \qquad \boxed{} \qquad \begin{array}{r} 5 \;\; 3 \\ \times \qquad 3 \\ \hline 1 \;\; 5 \;\; 9 \\ (\quad) \end{array} \qquad \boxed{}$$

Challenge and extension question

5 Fill in the boxes with suitable numbers to make the calculation true.

$$\begin{array}{r} \boxed{} \;\boxed{} \\ \times \qquad 8 \\ \hline \boxed{} \; 7 \;\; 2 \end{array}$$

9.6 Multiplying a two-digit number by a one-digit number (3)

Learning objective

Multiply two-digit numbers by one-digit numbers

Basic questions

1 Work these out mentally. Write the answers.

$2 \times 8 + 4 =$　　　$9 \times 3 + 3 =$　　　$6 \times 8 + 5 =$　　　$7 \times 7 + 4 =$

$8 \times 7 + 5 =$　　　$6 \times 6 + 5 =$　　　$9 \times 5 + 7 =$　　　$0 \times 8 + 3 =$

2 Use the column method to calculate.

(a) $77 \times 4 =$　　(b) $9 \times 36 =$　　(c) $25 \times 8 =$　　(d) $4 \times 75 =$

3 First estimate, and then calculate using the column method.

(a) $49 \times 7 =$

The product is between (　　) and (　　).

(b) $75 \times 6 =$

The product is between (　　) and (　　).

(c) $88 \times 8 =$

The product is between (　　) and (　　).

4 Is each of the following calculations correct? Put a $\checkmark$ for yes and a $\times$ for no in the bracket and make your correction in the box.

$$
\begin{array}{r}
9\ 9 \\
\times \qquad 9 \\
\hline
8\ 8\ 1 \\
(\qquad)
\end{array}
\qquad
\begin{array}{r}
2\ 6 \\
\times \qquad 8 \\
\hline
1\ 9\ 6 \\
(\qquad)
\end{array}
\qquad
\begin{array}{r}
6\ 8 \\
\times \qquad 5 \\
\hline
3\ 0\ 0 \\
(\qquad)
\end{array}
$$

5 Draw lines to match the calculations with the answers.

$25 \times 7 =$ $\qquad$ $56 \times 4 =$ $\qquad$ $9 \times 42 =$ $\qquad$ $5 \times 63 =$

315 $\qquad$ 378 $\qquad$ 224 $\qquad$ 175

6 Application problems.

(a) One 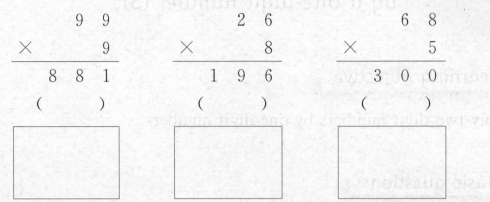 costs £98. How much do 4 toy motorbikes cost?

(b) One model sailing boat costs £57. How much do 6 model sailing boats cost?

 Challenge and extension question

7 Fill in the boxes with suitable numbers to make the calculation true.

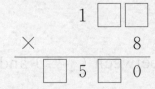

9.7 Multiplying a three-digit number by a one-digit number (1)

 Learning objective

Multiply three-digit numbers by one-digit numbers

 Basic questions

① Work these out mentally. Write the answers.

$3 \times 800 =$	$20 \times 8 =$	$900 \times 7 =$	$60 \times 6 =$
$3 \times 80 =$	$200 \times 8 =$	$90 \times 7 =$	$700 \times 4 =$
$3 \times 8 =$	$2 \times 8 =$	$9 \times 7 =$	$3 \times 9 =$

② Follow the example and split the numbers.

(a) $316 = 300 + 10 + 6$ (b) $427 = \underline{\quad} + \underline{\quad} + \underline{\quad}$

(c) $987 = \underline{\quad} + \underline{\quad} + \underline{\quad}$ (d) $634 = \underline{\quad} + \underline{\quad} + \underline{\quad}$

③ Work out these calculations. Show your working.

$$3 \times 316 =$$
$$3 \times \underline{\quad} = \underline{\quad}$$
$$3 \times \underline{\quad} = \underline{\quad}$$
$$3 \times \underline{\quad} = \underline{\quad}$$
$$\underline{\quad} + \underline{\quad} + \underline{\quad} =$$

$$3 \times 316 =$$

$$
\begin{array}{r}
3\ \ 1\ \ 6 \\
\times \qquad 3 \\
\hline
\end{array}
$$

④ Work out these calculations. Show your working.

$427 \times 4 =$ $634 \times 6 =$ $370 \times 5 =$

⑤ Use the columnar method to calculate.

   (a) $171 \times 7 =$ (b) $3 \times 279 =$ (c) $6 \times 309 =$

6 Is each of the following calculations correct? Put a $\checkmark$ for yes and a $\times$ for no in the bracket and make your correction in the box.

```
    2  3  5            1  0  7              6  7  2
 ×        4         ×        5          ×        8
 ─────────          ─────────           ────────────
    9  4  0            8  3  5            5  3  7  6
   (    )              (    )               (    )
```

Challenge and extension question

7 Think carefully to complete these.

   (a) Fill in the boxes with suitable numbers.

```
        4  1  6                    5  □  8
    ×         7                ×         □
    ─────────────             ─────────────
    □  □  □  2                 4  0  6  4
```

   (b) Find out the number that $\square$, $\triangle$ and $\bigcirc$ each stands for.

```
    □  △  ○  4              □ = (    )
 ×           3              △ = (    )
 ──────────────            ○ = (    )
    5  □  △  ○
```

9.8   Multiplying a three-digit number by a one-digit number (2)

Learning objective

Multiply three-digit numbers by one-digit numbers

Basic questions

① Work these out mentally. Write the answers.

$5 \times 5 =$ $2 \times 5 =$ $3 \times 7 =$ $9 \times 4 =$

$50 \times 5 =$ $20 \times 5 =$ $30 \times 7 =$ $90 \times 4 =$

$500 \times 5 =$ $200 \times 5 =$ $300 \times 7 =$ $900 \times 4 =$

② Look at the calculations and fill in the brackets.

```
    3  6  0                        3  6  0
×          4                    ×          4
─────────────                  ─────────────
□  □  □  □                      □  □  □  □
```

Multiplying 360 ones by 4   Multiplying 36 tens by 4

is (   ) ones.   is (   ) tens.

③ Use the column method to calculate. (First guess how many digits the product has.)

(a) $130 \times 6 =$ (b) $450 \times 9 =$ (c) $8 \times 250 =$

Is your guess before your calculation the same as your calculation result? Multiplying a three-digit number by a one digit number, the product could be a (-digit) number or a (-digit) number. Don't forget the zero(s) at the end of the number!

4 There are (   ) zeros at the end of product $4 \times 5 \times 5$.

There are (   ) zeros at the end of product $125 \times 8 \times 10$.

5 Application problems.

(a) John's mother finished reading a book in 9 days. She read 120 pages a day. How many pages are there in the book?

(b) There are 205 goats on a farm. There are 4 times as many sheep as there are goats. How many sheep are there?

Challenge and extension questions

6 Multiple choice question.

$24 \times \triangle = 2400 \times \star$. Comparing the relationship between $\triangle$ and $\star$, the conclusion is (   ).

A. $10 \times \triangle = \star$ B. $100 \times \star = \triangle$ C. $100 \times \triangle = \star$

D. $\star = \star$ E. $10 \times \star = \triangle$

7 Look at the table. First work out the product, and then compare how the product is changed in relation to the change of one of the numbers multiplied. What did you find?

A	400	400	800	800
B	3	6	3	6
A×B				

My finding: _____

9.9   Practice and exercise

Learning objective

Solve multiplication problems

Basic questions

1 Work these out mentally. Write the answers.

$9 \times 30 =$ $13 \times 7 =$ $2 \times 30 + 3 =$

$800 \times 5 =$ $16 \times 5 =$ $3 \times 30 - 27 =$

2 Use the column method to calculate.

$7 \times 42 =$ $6 \times 134 =$ $480 \times 7 =$

3 Fill in the $\bigcirc$ with $>$, $<$ or$=$.

(a) $604 \times 0 \bigcirc 236$ (b) $36 \times 6 \bigcirc 214$ (c) $37 + 3 \bigcirc 37 \times 3$

(d) $28 \times 8 \bigcirc 88 \times 2$ (e) $123 \times 4 \bigcirc 124 \times 3$ (f) $240 \times 5 \bigcirc 1200$

4 Fill in the brackets.

(a) There are (   ) zeros at the end of the product of 2500×8.

(b) The product of a one-digit number and a three-digit number could be a (-digit) number or a (-digit) number.

(c) The product of 49×5 is a (-digit) number. The product is between (   ) and (   ).

⑤ Write the number sentences and then calculate.

(a) What is the product of 650 multiplied by 7?

Number sentence: _____

(b) What is the sum of 4 seven hundred and twenty-threes?

Number sentence: _____

(c) What is 5 times 106?

Number sentence: _____

(d) Find the product of 38 and 8.

Number sentence: _____

⑥ Tom's weight is 39 kilograms. His father's weight is twice the weight of Tom's. What is his father's weight?

Answer: _____

⑦ John was reading a book. He read 18 pages per day for 9 days and still had 42 pages left. How many pages were there in the book?

Answer: _____

Challenge and extension questions

⑧ Some bookshelves were delivered to a school. Each bookshelf has 4 shelves and Mrs Lee put 26 books on each shelf. How many books did she put on 3 of the bookshelves?

Answer: _____

⑨ Fill in the boxes.

```
    7 □ 8                1  9 □
  ×    □              ×       □
  _____              _____
  □ □ 4 0              □ 6 0
```

9.10　Dividing whole tens and whole hundreds

Learning objective

Use division facts to divide multiples of 10 and 100

Basic questions

1 Simply facts.

$18 \div 6 = 3$	$24 \div 3 = 8$	$28 \div 4 = 7$	$6 \div 2 = 3$
$180 \div 6 = 30$	$240 \div 3 = 80$	$280 \div 4 = 70$	$600 \div 2 = 300$

Try it out on your own (i):

$8 \div 4 =$	$16 \div 4 =$	$32 \div 4 =$	$20 \div 4 =$
$80 \div 4 =$	$160 \div 4 =$	$320 \div 4 =$	$200 \div 4 =$

Try it out on your own (ii):

$9 \div 3 =$	$8 \div 2 =$	$5 \div 5 =$	$10 \div 5 =$
$90 \div 3 =$	$80 \div 2 =$	$50 \div 5 =$	$100 \div 5 =$
$900 \div 3 =$	$800 \div 2 =$	$500 \div 5 =$	$1000 \div 5 =$

2 The calculations can also be done this way. Fill in the brackets.

(　　) $\times 60 = 480$	(　　) $\times 70 = 560$	$80 \times ($　　$) = 720$
$480 \div 60 =$	$560 \div 70 =$	$720 \div 80 =$
$480 \div ($　　$) = 60$	$560 \div ($　　$) = 70$	$720 \div ($　　$) = 80$

3 Work out these calculations using your preferred way.

$400 \div 50 =$	$210 \div 7 =$	$540 \div 90 =$	$40 \div 2 =$
$400 \div 8 =$	$210 \div 30 =$	$540 \div 6 =$	$40 \div 20 =$
$120 \div 30 =$	$250 \div 50 =$	$150 \div 30 =$	$810 \div 90 =$
$360 \div 60 =$	$630 \div 90 =$	$490 \div 70 =$	$450 \div 90 =$

4 Write the number sentences and calculate.

(a) The dividend is 270 and divisor is 3. What is the quotient?

Number sentence: _____

(b) How many times 50 is 350?

Number sentence: _____

(c) Divide 640 into 8 parts equally. How much is each part?

Number sentence: _____

5 Application problems.

(a) A primary school received a donation of 720 books. If the books are shared equally by 9 classes, how many books does each class receive?

Answer: _____

(b) The price for a big screen TV is £1500. It is three times as much as the price for a small screen TV. How much does a small screen TV cost?

Answer: _____

(c) After 240 litres of cooking oil in a bottle were used, the amount of oil remaining in the bottle is 4 times the amount used. How many litres of oil were in the bottle at first?

Answer: _____

Challenge and extension question

6 What does each shape below stand for? Fill in the brackets.

$\triangle \times \square \times \bigcirc = 540$

$\triangle \times \square = 60$

$\square \times \bigcirc = 180$

$\triangle = (\quad)$ $\square = (\quad)$ $\bigcirc = (\quad)$

9.11   Dividing a two-digit number by a one-digit number (1)

Learning objective

Divide two-digit numbers by one-digit numbers

Basic questions

1. Work these out mentally. Write the answers.

   $9 \div 2 =$ $25 \div 4 =$ $27 \div 5 =$ $38 \div 6 =$

   $19 \div 3 =$ $36 \div 5 =$ $39 \div 4 =$ $47 \div 5 =$

2. Find the greatest number that will fill in each bracket.

   $6 \times (\quad) < 32$ $(\quad) \times 9 < 60$ $(\quad) \times 8 < 53$

   $8 \times (\quad) < 50$ $7 \times (\quad) < 62$ $(\quad) \times 9 < 78$

3. 5 children share 73 sweets equally. How many sweets can each child have?

   $$73 \div 5 = ?$$

   Mary's solution: $5 \times 10 = \boxed{}$ Joan's solution: $50 \div 5 = \boxed{}$

                       $50 \div 5 = \boxed{}$ $23 \div 5 = \boxed{}\ r\ \boxed{}$

                       $73 - 50 = \boxed{}$ $73 \div 5 = \boxed{}\ r\ \boxed{}$

                       $23 \div 5 = \boxed{}\ r\ \boxed{}$

                       $10 + 4 = \boxed{}$

                       $73 \div 5 = \boxed{}\ r\ \boxed{}$

4 Work these out.

$64 \div 4 =$	$92 \div 4 =$	$84 \div 7 =$	$81 \div 7 =$	$86 \div 6 =$
$40 \div 4 =$	$80 \div 4 =$			
$24 \div 4 =$	$12 \div 4 =$			

5 Write the number sentences and then calculate.

(a) When 95 is divided by 7, what are the quotient and remainder?

Number sentence: _____

(b) A number times 5 is 75. What is the number?

Number sentence: _____

(c) What number divided by 5 is 125?

Number sentence: _____

6 Application problems.

(a) The weight of a calf is 6 kg. The weight of a cow is 90 kg. How many times the weight of the cow is that of the calf?

Answer: _____

(b) A toy factory plans to make 96 toys in 4 days. If it makes 25 toys each day, can the target be met?

Answer: _____

Challenge and extension question

7 Write suitable signs from $+$, $-$, $\times$, $\div$ or ( ) into the following so the equations are true. The first one has been done for you.

$$4 + 4 - 4 - 4 = 0$$
$$4 \quad 4 \quad 4 \quad 4 = 1$$
$$4 \quad 4 \quad 4 \quad 4 = 2$$

$$4 \quad 4 \quad 4 \quad 4 = 3$$
$$4 \quad 4 \quad 4 \quad 4 = 5$$
$$4 \quad 4 \quad 4 \quad 4 = 8$$

9.12 Dividing a two-digit number by a one-digit number (2)

 Learning objective

Divide two-digit numbers by one-digit numbers

 Basic questions

1 Work these out mentally. Write the answers.

$20 \div 6 =$ $31 \div 5 =$ $63 \div 8 =$ $43 \div 7 =$

$75 \div 9 =$ $62 \div 7 =$ $48 \div 9 =$ $39 \div 4 =$

2 Use the column method to calculate. The first one has been done for you.

```
      1 5
   3) 4 5
      3
      ─
      1 5
      1 5
      ───
        0
```

```
   2) 7 8
```

```
   5) 6 5
```

```
   2) 4 6
```

```
   3) 9 3
```

```
   4) 4 8
```

3 Use the column method to calculate.

$84 \div 7 =$ $96 \div 3 =$ $68 \div 2 =$ $75 \div 3 =$

4 Write the number sentences and calculate.

(a) What is 39 divided 3?

Number sentence: _____

(b) What is 78 divided by 6?

Number sentence: _____

5 Application problems.

(a) There are 35 white rabbits and 53 grey rabbits. If one rabbit hutch can keep 4 rabbits, how many hutches are needed to keep all the rabbits?

(b) 54 children are playing group dancing and they are divided into 2 rows. How many children are there in each row?

 ## Challenge and extension questions

6 Fill in each box with 4, 11, 2 and 3 respectively.

$$\boxed{} \div \boxed{} = \boxed{} \ r \ \boxed{}$$

7 Lily's mother gave Lily 8 chocolates and gave the rest of the chocolates to Alice. The number of chocolates that Lily got was exactly half of the number Alice was given. How many chocolates did Alice get?

9.13 Dividing a two-digit number by a one-digit number (3)

Learning objective

Divide two-digit numbers by one-digit numbers

Basic questions

1 Find the greatest number that will fill in each bracket.

(   ) × 7 < 45   (   ) × 4 < 26   68 > 9 × (   )

3 × (   ) < 28   6 × (   ) < 35   47 > (   ) × 8

2 Write the answer for each of these. (Pay attention to the place where quotient is written.)

$6{\overline{\smash{)}3\,0}}$ $2{\overline{\smash{)}1\,9}}$ $9{\overline{\smash{)}3\,8}}$ $3{\overline{\smash{)}2\,0}}$

$6{\overline{\smash{)}3\,2}}$ $4{\overline{\smash{)}2\,1}}$ $8{\overline{\smash{)}2\,8}}$ $7{\overline{\smash{)}4\,0}}$

3 Use the column method to calculate.

27 ÷ 5 =   40 ÷ 6 =   58 ÷ 8 =   66 ÷ 9 =

$54 \div 3 =$ 　　　$65 \div 5 =$ 　　　$64 \div 4 =$ 　　　$72 \div 6 =$

4 Application problems.

(a) 27 children took part in a school boat modelling competition. They were divided into 3 groups. How many children were there in each group?

(b) 88 balls are put into 5 bags equally. How many balls are put into each bag? How many balls are left over?

(c) Each coat needs 5 buttons. How many coats can 78 buttons be sewn on to? How many buttons are left over?

Challenge and extension question

5 Mrs Lee brought some fancy erasers as prizes for the 6 winners of a mental calculation competition. She started by giving each winner one eraser and then continued to give the same number of erasers to each winner until she did not have enough erasers for every winner. The number of erasers left over is the same as the number of erasers each winner was given. How many erasers did Mrs Lee buy? (Give as many answers as you can think of.)

9.14 Dividing a two-digit number by a one-digit number (4)

Learning objective

Divide two-digit numbers by one-digit numbers

Basic questions

1 Work these out mentally. Write the answers.

$30 \div 3 =$ $40 \div 2 =$ $80 \div 4 =$ $500 \div 5 =$

$39 \div 3 =$ $48 \div 2 =$ $84 \div 4 =$ $6000 \div 3 =$

2 Work out these calculations. (Note the differences in the results.)

$96 \div 3 =$ $92 \div 3 =$ $96 \div 6 =$ $92 \div 6 =$

3 Use the column method to calculate.

$83 \div 4 =$ $81 \div 2 =$ $65 \div 6 =$ $60 \div 3 =$

$96 \div 9 =$ $53 \div 5 =$ $75 \div 7 =$ $87 \div 8 =$

4 Complete the tables.

(a)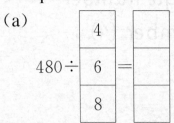

$480 \div$

4	
6	=
8	

(b)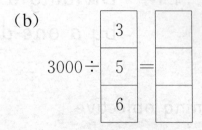

$3000 \div$

3	
5	=
6	

5 Work these out mentally. Write the answers.

$2 \times 200 =$ $300 \times 3 =$ $4 \times 500 =$

$400 \div 2 =$ $900 \div 3 =$ $2000 \div 4 =$

6 Write the number sentences and calculate.

(a) What is 82 divided by 2?

Number sentence: _____

(b) What is 900 divided by 3?

Number sentence: _____

(c) 640 is divided equally into 2 parts. How much is each part?

Number sentence: _____

(d) How many fours are there in 320?

Number sentence: _____

7 A patch of grassland of classroom size can produce enough oxygen daily for 3 people. How many patches of grassland of the same size are needed to produce enough oxygen daily for 210 people?

Number sentence: _____

 ## Challenge and extension question

8 An old monkey is playing a game with 12 little monkeys to help them learn maths.

The rules are as follows.

(1) All the 12 little monkeys line up.

(2) The little monkeys in the 1st, 3rd, 5th, 7th, 9th and 11th places are given one banana each and then leave. The other monkeys remain in the line.

(3) The little monkeys in the 1st, 3rd and 5th places in the new line are given two bananas each and then leave. The other monkeys again remain in the line.

(4) The little monkeys in the 1st and 3rd places in the line left are given 3 bananas each and leave the line.

(5) Finally, the remaining little money is given the final prize, that is, 5 bananas.

Question: If a monkey can choose any place in the line at the beginning, what place do you think it should choose in order to receive the final prize?

9.15 Dividing a two-digit number by a one-digit number (5)

 Learning objective

Divide two-digit numbers by one-digit numbers

 Basic questions

1 Work these out mentally. Write the answers.

$30 \times 2 =$ $120 \times 3 =$ $9000 \div 3 =$ $2000 \times 4 =$

$46 \div 2 =$ $300 \times 5 =$ $60 \div 9 =$ $1000 \times 7 =$

$21 \times 3 =$ $840 \div 4 =$ $240 \div 6 =$ $2000 \div 5 =$

2 Use the column method to calculate. Check your answers.

$58 \div 4 =$ $61 \div 2 =$ $92 \div 5 =$

$37 \div 3 =$ $97 \div 6 =$ $74 \div 7 =$

3 Application problems.

(a) There are 96 sheep and 3 horses on a farm. By how many times is the number of the horse the number of the sheep?

(b) A book has 63 pages. Tim is reading 7 pages a day. In how many days will he finish the book?

(c) Mary helps her mother to ice some cupcakes. She ices 8 cupcakes every minute. How many minutes does she need to ice 96 cupcakes?

(d) 39 girls and 45 boys from Year 3 went to work in an orchard. They were divided into groups of 4. How many groups were they divided into?

(e) John put 45 sweets into 15 sweet jars. He put 5 sweets in each jar. Did he have enough sweet jars? If yes, how many sweet jars were left over?

 Challenge and extension questions

4 Use the four digits 3, 4, 7 and 31 to write division sentences with remainders. Write as many as you can.

5 Fill in the boxes.

$\boxed{} \div 7 = 5 \text{ r } 4$ $\qquad$ $\boxed{} \div \boxed{} = 8 \text{ r } 7$

9.16 Dividing a three-digit number by a one-digit number (1)

Learning objective

Divide three-digit numbers by one-digit numbers

Basic questions

1. Work these out mentally. Write the answers.

$160 \div 8 =$ $300 \div 6 =$ $200 \div 5 =$ $1600 \div 8 =$

$3000 \div 6 =$ $2000 \div 5 =$ $220 \div 2 =$ $840 \div 4 =$

2. 597 books are given to 4 classes equally. How many books does each class get? How many books are left over?

$$597 \div 4 = ?$$

Method 1:   Method 2: Use the column method

Since $400 \div 4 =$

         $160 \div 4 =$

         $37 \div 4 =$

We have: $597 \div 4 =$

Answer: Each class can get _____ books, and _____ books are left over. (Can you check if the answer is correct?)

3. Complete these calculations.

$637 \div 3 =$	$665 \div 5 =$	$738 \div 6 =$
$600 \div 3 =$	$500 \div 5 =$	
$30 \div 3 =$	$150 \div 5 =$	
$7 \div 3 =$	$15 \div 5 =$	

4 Use the column method to calculate.

$$4\overline{)\,5\ 3\ 6}$$ $$7\overline{)\,8\ 5\ 6}$$ $$8\overline{)\,9\ 3\ 4}$$

5 Application problems.

(a) A group of children picked 266 apples from the apple trees in the school's garden. 62 apples were reserved for visitors. The rest were shared equally by the 6 classes in Year 1. How many apples did each class get?

(b) A school bought 4 boxes of books. Each box has 100 books. How many books did school buy in total? If the books are given to 5 year groups (from Year 1 to Year 5) equally, how many books will each year group receive?

Challenge and extension question

6 Find the value of $\triangle$ and fill in the brackets.

$$\triangle + \triangle = (\qquad)$$
$$\triangle - \triangle = (\qquad)$$
$$\triangle \times \triangle = (\qquad)$$
$$\underline{+\ \triangle \div \triangle = (\qquad)}$$
$$100 \qquad\qquad \triangle = (\qquad)$$

9.17 Dividing a three-digit number by a one-digit number (2)

 Learning objective

Divide three-digit numbers by one-digit numbers

 Basic questions

1 Work these out mentally. Write the answers.

$80 \div 4 =$ $600 \div 6 =$ $510 - 480 =$ $39 \div 3 =$

$900 \div 3 =$ $60 - 37 =$ $23 \times 4 =$ $25 \times 6 =$

2 Find the greatest number that will fill in each bracket.

$6 \times \boxed{} < 38$ $5 \times \boxed{} < 32$ $8 \times \boxed{} < 85$

$4 \times \boxed{} < 25$ $7 \times \boxed{} < 60$ $3 \times \boxed{} < 17$

3 Try it out on your own.

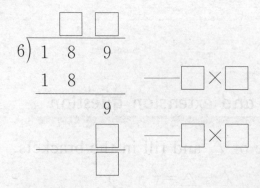

4 First decide how many digits the quotient has and then calculate.

$3 \overline{)\,6\ 2\ 4}$ $8 \overline{)\,9\ 3\ 6}$ $2 \overline{)\,3\ 2\ 1}$ $4 \overline{)\,5\ 6\ 3\ 6}$

⑤ Complete these calculations and then check the answers.

$656 \div 6 =$ $\qquad$ $736 \div 9 =$ $\qquad$ $496 \div 7 =$ $\qquad$

⑥ Application problems.

(a) A dragonfly eats 4200 mosquitoes in a week. How many mosquitoes does it eat per day?

Answer: _____

(b) 480 toy cars were equally placed into 5 big boxes. How many toy cars were placed into each big box?

Answer: _____

If the toy cars in each big box were put into 8 small boxes equally, how many toy cars were in each small box?

Answer: _____

Challenge and extension questions

⑦ Think carefully. Which group do the following numbers belong to? Write the numbers in the correct circles.

345   630   934   616   147   299   373

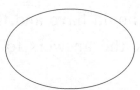 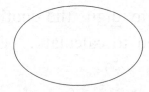 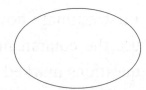

Divided by 2 and the remainder is 0

Divided by 3 and the remainder is 1

Divided by 7 and the remainder is 5

⑧ Tom was picking apples in an orchard. He picked 304 apples in 4 hours. Joan picked 36 apples in half an hour. Who did the apple picking faster? (How many ways can you think of to compare? Try to show two ways of your working.)

9.18   Dividing a three-digit number by a one-digit number (3)

Learning objective

Divide three-digit numbers by one-digit numbers

Basic questions

1 Look at the number sentences in the first column and then complete the number sentences in the second column.
(a) $128 \times 7 = 896$ $896 \div 7 =$
(b) $7254 \div 9 = 806$ $806 \times 9 =$

2 Correct each calculation if it contains mistake.

$354 \div 6 = 59$ $663 \div 7 = 99$ $428 \div 4 = 107$

3 First estimate how many digits the quotient should have and then use the column method to calculate. (Check the answers to the questions marked with * .)

$380 \div 3 =$ $843 \div 6 =$ * $709 \div 7 =$

* $450 \div 6 =$ $750 \div 5 =$ $919 \div 9 =$

4 Fill in the brackets.

(   ) $\times 7 = 266$ $9 \times ($ $) = 486$

(   ) $\div 6 = 350$ $384 \div ($ $) = 8$

5 True or false.

(a) 0 divided by any non-zero number is zero.   (   )

(b) For division $\boxed{} 0 \boxed{} \div 4$, only when the digit in the hundreds place of the dividend is 4, can the digit in the tens place of the quotient be zero.   (   )

(c) If the divisor is a one-digit number and the dividend is a three-digit number with 0 in its tens place, then the number in the tens place of the quotient must be zero.   (   )

(d) If ● $\div$ ▲ $= 101$ r 8, then ▲ $=9$, ● $=909$.   (   )

6 A school has bought 504 pots of flowers and plans to place them in rows. Each row must have the same number of pots. Can you design a few ways to do so? Fill in the brackets and then write the number sentences.

Plan 1: Put (   ) pots for each row for (   ) rows.

Number sentence: _____

Plan 2: Put (   ) pots for each row for (   ) rows.

Number sentence: _____

Plan 3: Put (   ) pots for each row for (   ) rows.

Number sentence: _____

Challenge and extension question

7 Two school buildings are 80 metres apart. If one pot of flowers is placed every 2 metres, how many pots of flowers are needed to cover the distance from one building to the other?

9.19   Application of division

Learning objective

Use division to solve practical problems

Basic questions

1 Work these out mentally. Write the answers.

$17 \div 3 =$ $33 \div 7 =$ $43 \div 8 =$ $29 \div 9 =$

$52 \div 6 =$ $75 \div 10 =$ $25 \div 4 =$ $42 \div 5 =$

2 Fill in the brackets.

(a) When 618 is divided by 5, the quotient is (   ) and the remainder is (   ).

(b) To see if $251 \div 3 = 83$ r 2 is correct, you can use (   ) $\times$ (   ) + (   ) = (   ) to check.

(c) There are (   ) zeros at the end of the product of 800×5.

(d) In a division sentence, if both the dividend and divisor are the same, then the quotient is (   ). If the dividend and the quotient are the same, then the divisor is (   ). If the quotient is to be 0, the dividend is (   ).

3 Application problems.

(a) A group of children plan to put 140 kg of peanuts into boxes. Each box can hold 6 kg. At least how many boxes are needed?

(b) Two Year 3 classes go rowing. Each boat can seat 7 children. There are 29 children in Class One and 32 children in Class Two. How many boats are needed for each class separately?

If the classes share the boats, how many boats are needed?

(c) Tom has £50 to buy some pencil boxes. Each pencil box costs £8. How many pencil boxes can he buy?

(d) Joan has 147 pieces of paper. 8 pieces of paper are needed to make one exercise book. How many exercise books can she make with the 147 pieces of paper?

With the remaining pieces of paper, how many more pieces are needed to make another exercise book?

 ## Challenge and extension questions

4 A company uses 3 kilograms of fresh fish to make 1 kilogram of dried fish. How many kilograms of dried fish can it make using 750 kilograms of fresh fish?

5 One day a mother asked her daughter: "A piece of wood is sawn into 7 pieces. It takes 5 minutes to saw each piece. How long does it take to saw the 7 pieces?" The daughter answered without hesitation: "5 minutes for 1 piece, of course — it takes 35 minutes to saw 7 pieces." "No, it takes 30 minutes," mother said. Is mother right?

9.20 Finding the total price

Learning objective

Use division to solve practical problems

Basic questions

1 Work these out mentally. Write the answers.

$21 \times 3 =$	$80 \div 5 =$	$16 \times 2 =$	$40 \times 3 - 40 =$
$7200 \div 6 =$	$20 \times 4 =$	$180 + 70 =$	$49 \div 7 + 8 =$
$13 \times 7 =$	$90 - 26 =$	$270 \div 9 =$	$48 \div 3 + 56 =$

2 Complete the table.

	Pencil box	Pen	Coloured pencil (in box)
Unit price (price per item)	£6		£9 per box
Quantity (number of items)	7	10	
Total price		£340	£900

3 Fill in the ◯ with × or ÷ and the brackets with "total price", "unit price" or "quantity".

Unit price ◯ (　　) = Total price

Total price ◯ (　　) = Quantity

Total price ◯ (　　) = Unit price

4 John's mother bought 4 dresses. Each dress costs £105. How much did she spend in total?

⑤ There are 24 apples in a box. The price for each box of apples is £30. What is the total price for 3 of the boxes? How many apples are there in 8 boxes?

6 Write the number sentences and calculate.
　(a) What is 6 times 660?
　　　Number sentence: _____
　(b) How many times 6 is 660?
　　　Number sentence: _____
　(c) When the divisor is 8, the quotient is 402 and the remainder is 7, what is the dividend?
　　　Number sentence: _____

⑦ A box can hold 8 basketballs. How many boxes can hold 768 basketballs?

Challenge and extension questions

8 A school has planted 12 trees along one side of the road from one end to the other. One tree was planted every 6 metres. How long is the road?

⑨ It took Mark 5 minutes to walk from the 1st tree to the 6th tree along the main path in a school. At which tree was he after 15 minutes if he walked at the same pace?

Unit test 9

1 Work these out mentally. Write the answers.

$8 \times 30 =$	$40 \times 40 =$	$24 \times 5 - 100 =$	$7 \times 8 + 45 =$
$300 \times 6 =$	$50 \div 10 =$	$8 \times 2 \times 4 =$	$80 \div 4 - 17 =$
$540 + 5 =$	$200 \div 4 =$	$400 \div 8 =$	$170 + 130 =$
$5400 \div 6 =$	$360 \div 4 =$	$8 \times 2 + 12 =$	$48 \div 8 + 9 =$

2 Use the column method to calculate. (Check the answer to the question marked with ∗.)

(a) $4 \times 276 =$ (b) $780 \div 6 =$ (c) ∗$919 \div 9 =$

3 Work out these calculations, step by step.

(a) $182 \times 5 + 318$ (b) $456 \div 8 \times 4$ (c) $25 \times 4 + 175$

4 Write the number sentences and then calculate.

(a) 4 times a number is 520. What is the number?

Number sentence: _____

(b) What is the sum of 4 times 38 and the greatest two-digit number?

Number sentence: _____

(c) The divisor is 7, the quotient is 192 and the remainder is 2. What is the dividend?

Number sentence: _____

(d) How many threes are there in 69?

Number sentence: _____

5 Fill in the brackets.

(a) The product of 48×6 is between (　　) and (　　), nearer to (　　).

(b) The product of the least three-digit number and the greatest two-digit number is (　　).

(c) $23 \times 6 = ($　$) \times 6 + ($　$) + 6 = ($　$)$
    $126 \times 4 = ($　$) \times 4 + ($　$) \times 4 + ($　$) \times 4 = ($　$)$.

(d) In $472 \div 8$, the greatest place of value of the quotient is in the (　　) place. It is a (　　)-digit number.

(e) To make the quotient of $\boxed{}45 \div 5$ a three-digit number, the least possible number in the $\boxed{}$ is (　　). If the quotient is a two-digit number, the greatest possible number in the $\boxed{}$ is (　　).

(f) $829 \div ($　$) = 5$ r 4

(g) There are 20 red flowers. It is twice the number of yellow flowers. The total number of red flowers and yellow flowers is (　　).

(h) In $\boxed{} \div \boxed{} = 16$ r 7. The least possible number of the divisor is (　　) and accordingly, the dividend is (　　).

(i) There are (　　) zeros at the end of the product 2400×5.

6 A school bought 8 computers. Each computer costs £650. How much did the school pay in total for the computers?

7 Tom and his 3 friends collected 634 empty bottles in a school environment campaign. If they put them into 8 bags equally, how many bottles were there in each bag? How many empty bottles were left over?

8 Tim has 741 pieces of paper to make exercise books. 9 pieces of paper are needed to make one exercise book. How many exercise books can he make with the 741 pieces? With the remaining pieces of paper, how many more pieces are needed to make another exercise book?

9 A fruit shop has 200 kg of watermelons. It is 5 times the amount of apples. How many more kilograms of watermelons does the shop have than that of apples?

10 A group of children need to make 400 red flowers for a nursery. They have made 260 red flowers. The rest of the flowers must be made in two days. How many flowers do they need to make each day, on average, in the next two days?

11 A toy factory has made 252 boxes of blocks in the past 9 days. Now it is making 35 boxes each day. How many more boxes of blocks does it make, on average, each day now than before?

12 The weight of Alvin's father is 4 times that of Alvin. Alvin's weight is 24 kg. What is the weight of Alvin's father? How many more kilograms heavier is he than Alvin?

13 In the number sentence, each ★ stands for the same digit. What digit does ★ stand for in order to make the number sentence correct?

$$1★ + ★1 + ★ = 11★$$
$$★ = (\quad\quad)$$

Chapter 10　Let's practise geometry

10.1　Angles

 Learning objective

Identify and explore angles

Basic questions

1 How many angles are there in each shape? Fill in the brackets.

(　　) angles　(　　) angles　(　　) angles　(　　) angles

2 True or false.

(a) Every geometric shape must have at least one angle.　(　　)

(b) The wider the two sides of an angle are open, the greater the angle is.　(　　)

(c) All right angles are equal.　(　　)

(d) Two right angles make a half turn.　(　　)

3 Multiple choice questions.

(a) In the angles below, the greatest angle is (　　).

　　A.　　　　　　B.　　　　　　C.　　　　　　D.

(b) When the hour hand and the minute hand on a clock face

form a right angle, it could be (　　).

A. 12 o'clock　　　　　　B. half past 3

C. 6 o'clock　　　　　　D. 9 o'clock

(c) How many right angles make a complete turn?

A. one　　　　B. two　　　　C. three　　　　D. four

4 How many angles are there in each shape? How many are right angles? Fill in the brackets.

(　) angles　　　　(　) angles　　　　(　) angles　　　　(　) angles

(　) right angles　(　) right angles　(　) right angles　(　) right angles

(　) angles　　　　(　) angles　　　　(　) angles　　　　(　) angles

(　) right angles　(　) right angles　(　) right angles　(　) right angles

5 Draw three angles as indicated in the grid below.

(a) a right angle

(b) an angle that is less than a right angle (or called "an acute angle")

(c) an angle that is greater than a right angle (or called "an obtuse angle")

Challenge and extension questions

6 Draw a line on the shape so that it has 3 more right angles.

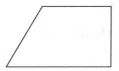

7 A square has 4 angles. If one of its four corners is cut off, how many angles will there be in the remaining part? (Hands-on: You may draw squares on paper and then cut them out accordingly.)

10.2 Identifying different types of lines (1)

 Learning objective

Identify horizontal and vertical lines

 Basic questions

1 Draw lines to match.

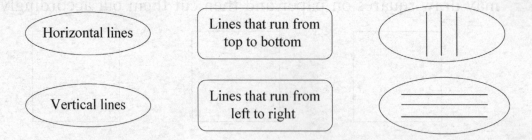

Horizontal lines

Vertical lines

Lines that run from top to bottom

Lines that run from left to right

2 Look at the shapes and write the numbers of the vertical lines and horizontal lines on the answer lines.

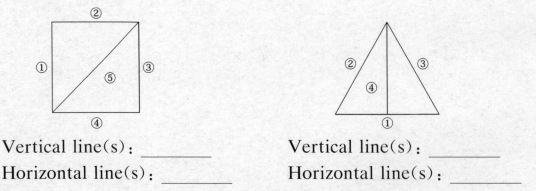

Vertical line(s): _____   Vertical line(s): _____
Horizontal line(s): _____   Horizontal line(s): _____

3 The picture below shows one side of a house. Identify all the horizontal lines and vertical lines. Then use numbers to denote these lines and write them below.

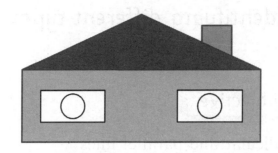

Vertical lines: _____

Horizontal lines: _____

4 True or false.

(a) After a quarter turn, a horizontal line is still a horizontal line.　　　　　　　　　　　　　　　　　　　　　　　(　)

(b) After a half turn, a vertical line will turn to be a horizontal line.　　　　　　　　　　　　　　　　　　　　　　　　(　)

(c) After a three quarter turn, a horizontal line will turn to be a vertical line.　　　　　　　　　　　　　　　　　　　　　(　)

(d) After a complete turn, a vertical line is still a vertical line.
　　　　　　　　　　　　　　　　　　　　　　　　　　(　)

Challenge and extension question

5 Write two to four examples of vertical lines and horizontal lines from your daily life. (Hint: you may look around your home, classroom or environment.)

_____

_____

10.3 Identifying different types of lines (2)

 Learning objective

Identify perpendicular and parallel lines

 Basic questions

1 Draw lines to match.

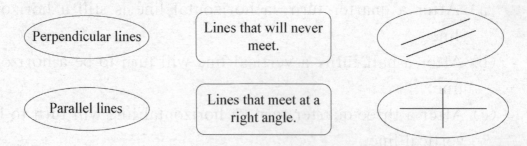

2 Identify parallel lines and/or perpendicular lines in each shape. Use numbers to denote these lines in the shape and write them on the answer lines. Write "none" if you cannot identify any.

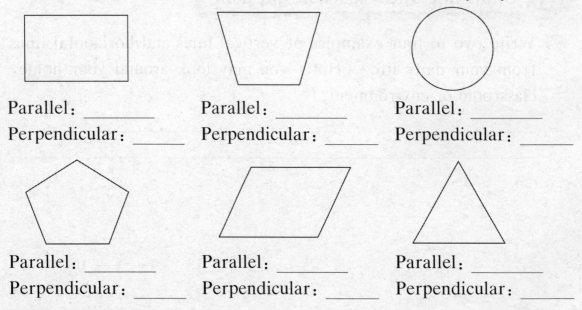

Parallel: _____   Parallel: _____   Parallel: _____
Perpendicular: _____   Perpendicular: _____   Perpendicular: _____

Parallel: _____   Parallel: _____   Parallel: _____
Perpendicular: _____   Perpendicular: _____   Perpendicular: _____

3 Look at the ladder and identify the types of lines shown for a, b, c, d and e. (Hint: use "horizontal", "vertical", "parallel" and "perpendicular" to fill in the brackets.)

(a) Lines a and b are (   ) lines.

They are also (   ) lines.

(b) Lines c, d and e are (   ) lines.

They are also (   ) lines.

(c) Lines a and c are (   ) lines.

(d) Lines a and d are (   ) lines.

(e) Lines b and e are (   ) lines.

4 True or false.

(a) Two horizontal lines are parallel.   (   )

(b) Two vertical lines are perpendicular to each other.   (   )

(c) Two perpendicular lines will meet at a point.   (   )

(d) Two lines are either parallel or perpendicular.   (   )

Challenge and extension question

5 Write two to four examples of parallel lines and perpendicular lines from your daily life. (Hint: you may look around your home, classroom or environment).

_____

_____

10.4 Drawing 2-D shapes and making 3-D shapes

 Learning objective

Explore properties of 2-D and 3-D shapes

 Basic questions

1 Complete the table. The first row has been done for you.

	Is it a 2-D or 3-D shape?	What is the name of the shape?	If it is a 2-D shape, is it a symmetrical figure?
	2-D	triangle	no

2 Use a straight edge to draw the 2-D shapes.

(a) a rectangle   (b) a pentagon   (c) an octagon

3 Use the 1-cm square dot grids to draw the shapes with the given conditions.
  (a) A triangle with (1) one angle being a right angle and (2) the lengths of its two sides being 2 cm and 3 cm each.

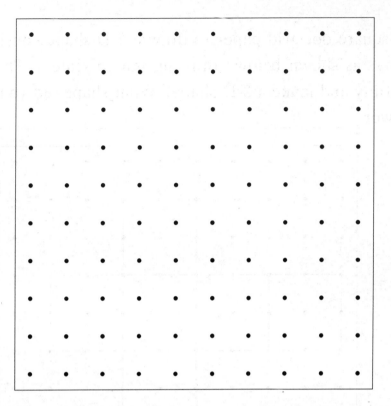

(b) A hexagon with （1） two sides being parallel and （2） the lengths of the two parallel sides being 1 cm and 5 cm each.

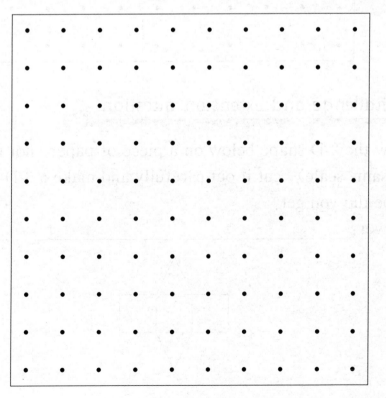

4 Use square dot grid paper to draw a 2-D shape consisting of five squares as shown below (drawing not to scale). Then cut it out carefully and make a 3-D shape. What shape did you get?

Answer: _____

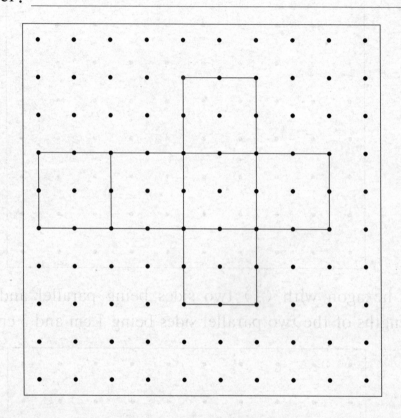

 Challenge and extension question

5 Draw the 2-D shape below on a piece of paper (not necessarily to the same scale), cut it out carefully and make a 3-D shape. What shape did you get?

Answer: _____

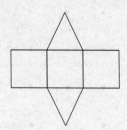

10.5 Length: metre, centimetre and millimetre

 Learning objective

Measure and compare lengths using metres, centimetres and millimetres

Basic questions

1. Fill in the brackets.

   1 m = (   )cm   1 cm = (   )mm   1 m = (   )mm

   $\frac{1}{2}$ m = (   )cm   15 cm = (   )mm   700 cm = (   )m

   1 m and 30 cm = (   )cm   2 m and 26 cm = (   )cm

   $\frac{3}{10}$ cm = (   )mm   900 mm = (   )cm

2. Measure each object and fill in the brackets.

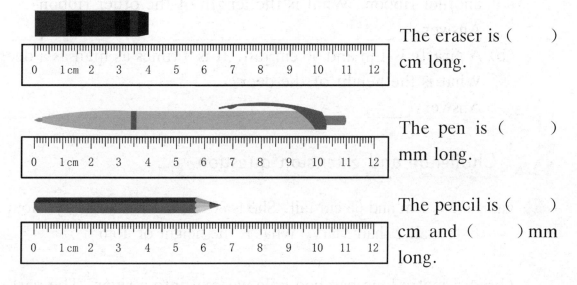

The eraser is (   ) cm long.

The pen is (   ) mm long.

The pencil is (   ) cm and (   ) mm long.

3. Write a suitable unit in each bracket.
   (a) A dining table is about 80 (   ) high.
   (b) A nail is about 50 (   ) long.

(c) A giraffe is about 5 (   ) tall.

(d) The length of a bus is about 10 (   ).

(e) A UK passport photo size is 45 (   ) high by 35 (   ) wide.

4 Fill in the brackets with >, < or =.

(a) 810 cm(   )8 m   (b) 7 m(   )75 cm

(c) 1 m(   )100 mm   (d) 5 cm(   )500 mm

(e) 6 m and 57 cm(   )675 cm   (f) 360 cm(   )3 m and 600 mm

(g) 28 m+500 cm(   )33 m   (h) 1 m+60 mm(   )106 cm

5 Write the following in order, from the least to the greatest, using <.

(a) 340 cm, 12 m, 11m 98cm, 1000 cm, 300 mm

Answer:_____

(b) 50 m, 490 mm, 4 m and 90 cm, 600 cm,

Answer:_____

6 Application problems.

(a) A ribbon is 805 cm long. It is 1 m and 5 mm longer than another ribbon. What is the length of the other ribbon?

Answer:_____

(b) A giraffe is 4 m and 50 cm tall. It is 5 times as high as a deer. What is the height of the deer?

Answer:_____

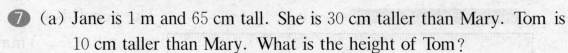

Challenge and extension question

7 (a) Jane is 1 m and 65 cm tall. She is 30 cm taller than Mary. Tom is 10 cm taller than Mary. What is the height of Tom?

(b) A 5-metre long bamboo pole was put into a river. The part of the pole above the water was 200 cm and the part of the pole inserted in the mud at the bottom was 90 mm. How deep was the water in the river?

10.6   Perimeters of simple 2-D shapes (1)

 Learning objective

Calculate and measure the perimeters of simple 2-D shapes

 Basic questions

1. Use a coloured pen to trace the borderline of each figure below.

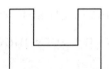 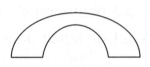 

2. Find the perimeter of each figure on the 1-m square grid paper.

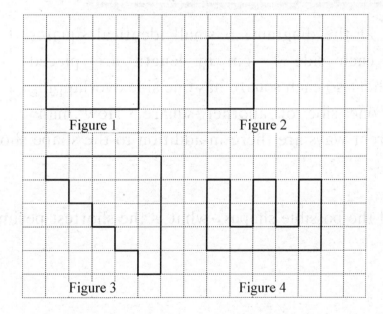

Figure 1: The perimeter is _____.

Figure 2: The perimeter is _____.

Figure 3: The perimeter is _____.

Figure 4: The perimeter is _____.

3 Find the perimeters of the following figures (drawing not to scale).

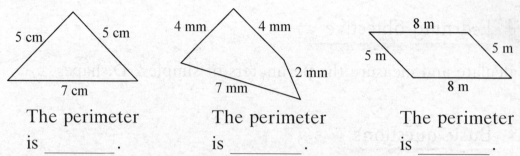

5 cm 5 cm
7 cm

The perimeter is _____.

4 mm 4 mm
2 mm
7 mm

The perimeter is _____.

8 m
5 m 5 m
8 m

The perimeter is _____.

4 Every morning Mr Lowe runs 6 laps on a path around a pond near his house. The pond is a pentagon shape and each side of the path is 30 metres long. What distance does he run every morning?

Answer: _____

Challenge and extension question

5 Look at the diagram. 5 small identical squares with each side 1 cm in length are pieced together, so each square has one side overlapping with one side of another square. How many different ways are there in addition to the shape shown?

In all the possible shapes, what is the shortest perimeter?

10.7 Perimeters of simple 2-D shapes (2)

 Learning objective

Calculate and measure the perimeters of simple 2-D shapes

 Basic questions

1. In each shape, the length of one side of each small square is 1 cm. Find its perimeter.

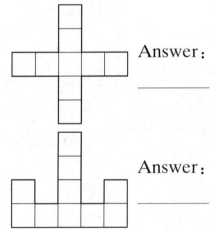

Answer:

_____

Answer:

_____

Answer:

_____

Answer:

_____

2. Calculate the perimeters of the following figures. (Drawing not to scale.)

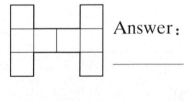

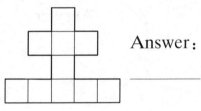

Answer: _____

Answer: _____

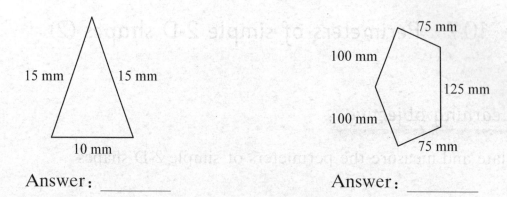

15 mm   15 mm

10 mm

Answer: _____

75 mm

100 mm

125 mm

100 mm

75 mm

Answer: _____

3 Measure each figure below and find its perimeter. Write the number sentence you use to get your result. (unit: mm)

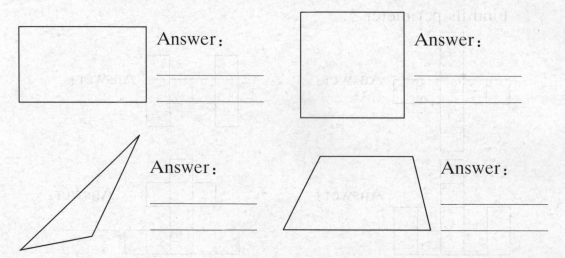

Answer:

_____

_____

Answer:

_____

_____

Answer:

_____

_____

Answer:

_____

_____

4 Look at the diagram. An ant is walking along the lines of an 8-cm square grid from Point A to Point B. How many centimetres must the ant walk at least to reach Point B?

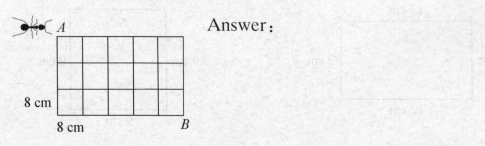

A

8 cm

8 cm   B

Answer:

Challenge and extension questions

5 The figure below shows a rectangle. A curve connecting A and B divides the rectangle into two shapes. Does Shape 1 have a longer perimeter? Give your reason.

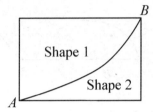

Answer: _____ (write "yes" or "no")

Reason: _____

_____

6 How long is the perimeter of each figure below (unit: mm)? Write the number sentence you use to get your result.

(a)

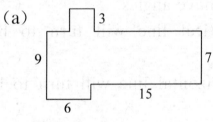

Answer:

(b)

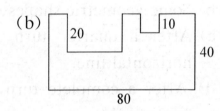

Answer:

Unit test 10

1 Are all of the following angles? Write each number that shows an angle and a right angle on the answer lines below.

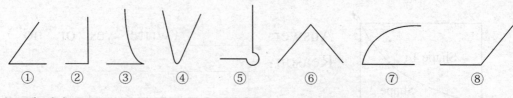

① ② ③ ④ ⑤ ⑥ ⑦ ⑧

Angle(s): _____ Right angle(s): _____

2 True or false.

(a) All right angles are equal. ( )

(b) Some geometric shapes do not have angles. ( )

(c) After a quarter turn, a vertical line will turn to be a horizontal line. ( )

(d) After a complete turn, a horizontal line will turn to be a vertical line. ( )

(e) Two perpendicular lines meet at a right angle. ( )

(f) If two lines are not parallel, they must be perpendicular. ( )

(g) The length of one whole round of a tree leaf is the perimeter of the leaf. ( )

(h) If the three sides of a triangle are 3 cm, 4 cm and 5 cm long, its perimeter is 60 cm. ( )

3 Look at the picture and fill in the brackets with "horizontal", "vertical", "parallel" or "perpendicular".

(a) Lines *a*, *b*, *c* and *d* are ( ) lines.

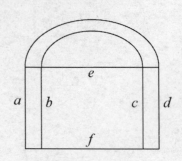

They are also (   ) lines.

(b) Lines *e* and *f* are (   ) lines.

They are also (   ) lines.

(c) Lines *a* and *f* are (   ) lines.

(d) Lines *a* and *e* are (   ) lines.

(e) Lines *b* and *f* are (   ) lines.

4 Fill in the brackets.

$8 \text{ m} = ($ $) \text{cm}$ $1 \text{ m} = ($ $) \text{mm}$ $900 \text{ mm} = ($ $) \text{cm}$

$\frac{1}{2} \text{ cm} = ($ $) \text{mm}$ $100 \text{ cm} = ($ $) \text{mm}$ $1000 \text{ cm} = ($ $) \text{ m}$

$\frac{1}{4} \text{ m} = ($ $) \text{mm}$ $5 \text{ m and } 66 \text{ cm} = ($ $) \text{cm}$

$880 \text{ cm} = ($ $) \text{ m and } ($ $) \text{cm}$ $\frac{9}{10} \text{ cm} = ($ $) \text{mm}$

5 Multiple choice questions.

(a) The figure that shows a right angle is (   ).

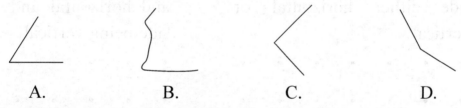

     A.   B.   C.   D.

(b) Each side of a square is 4 cm long. Its perimeter is (   ).

     A. 4 cm   B. 8 cm   C. 12 cm   D. 16 cm

(c) 9 squares with one side of 1-cm length are put together to form the following figures. The figure that has the shortest perimeter is (   ).

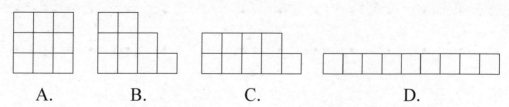

     A.   B.   C.   D.

(d) Look at the diagram and compare the perimeters of Graph A and Graph B. The correct conclusion is (   ).

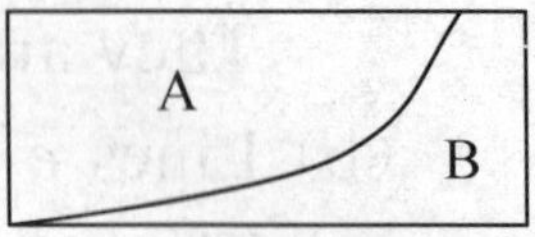

A. They are equal.

B. The perimeter of Graph A is greater than that of Graph B.

C. The perimeter of Graph A is shorter than the perimeter of Graph B.

D. Not sure.

6 Count the angles in the diagram. There are (   ) angles.

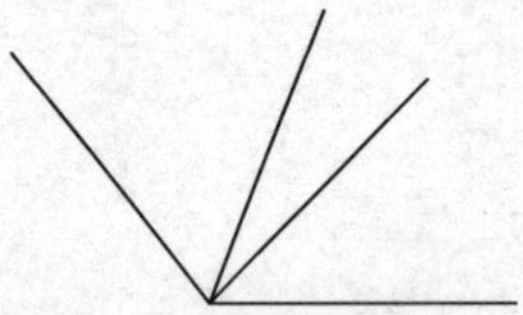

7 Use the 1-cm square dot grids to draw the shapes with the given conditions.

(a) A square with (1) each side being 3 cm long and (2) each side either horizontal or vertical.

(b) A pentagon with (1) the bottom side being 3 cm long and horizontal and (2) no side being vertical.

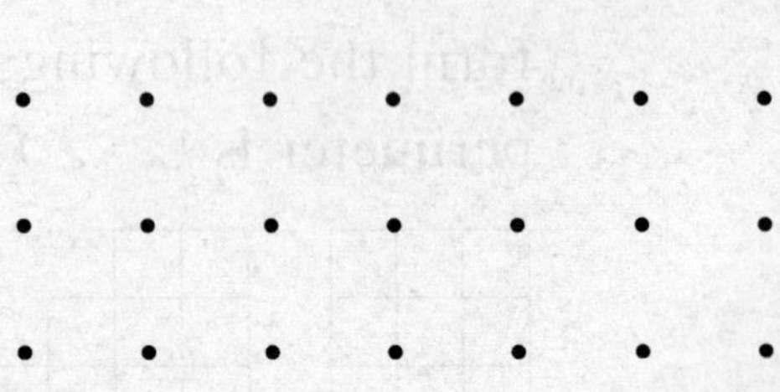

8 Look at the shaded figure on the 1-m square grid (drawing not to scale). What is the perimeter of the shaded figure?

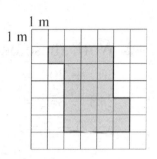

9 Measure each figure and find its perimeter. Write the number sentence you use to get your result. (unit: mm)

Answer:
_____
_____

Answer:
_____
_____

Answer:
_____
_____

10 Tom accidently spilled ink over some rectangular graph paper as shown in the figure (drawing not to scale). Given that the length of one side of each small square is 2 cm, how long is the perimeter of the original paper?

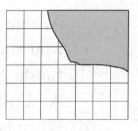

11 Every day, Jim runs 3 complete laps around a hexagonal path near his home. Each side of the hexagonal path is 90 metres long. How many metres does Jim run every day?

End of year test

1 Work these out mentally. Write the answers. （12%）

$600+200=$ $150-90=$ $24\times5=$ $54\div9=$

$248+352=$ $835-738=$ $270\div3=$ $770\div7=$

$6\times9+7=$ $7\times6\times0=$ $7\times5\times2=$ $25\times4+105=$

2 Work out these calculations. （6%）

(a) $\dfrac{1}{5}+\dfrac{3}{5}=$ (b) $\dfrac{5}{9}-\dfrac{2}{9}=$ (c) $1-\dfrac{1}{6}=$

(d) $\dfrac{5}{11}+\dfrac{3}{11}=$ (e) $\dfrac{3}{8}-\dfrac{3}{8}=$ (f) $\dfrac{4}{7}+0=$

3 Multiple choice questions. （8%）

(a) The product of two sevens is (　　).

     A. 27   B. 14   C. 49   D. unknown

(b) (　　) of the following figures show that in each figure the shaded part is $\dfrac{1}{4}$ of the whole figure.

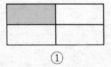 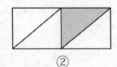 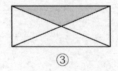 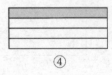

     ①   ②   ③   ④

     A. one   B. two   C. three   D. all

(c) Kim started lunch at five to twelve and took 32 minutes to finish. She finished at (　　).

     A. 12:32   B. 12:27   C. 11:23   D. 12:37

(d) When both the divisor and the quotient are 9, the dividend is (　　).

     A. 9   B. 18   C. 27   D. 81

4 Fill in the brackets. （16%）

(a) 1 m＝(   )cm＝(   )mm

(b) Write a suitable unit in each bracket.

   (i) Tom's weight is 30 (   ).

   (ii) Joan did 15 skips in 5 (   ).

   (iii) A textbook costs 7 (   ).

   (iv) In a common year, there are 28 (   ) in February.

(c) After a 1-metre long string is folded in half twice, each part is (   ) of the string. It is (   ) metre long.

(d) $\dfrac{2}{3} = \dfrac{4}{(\quad)} = \dfrac{(\quad)}{12}$.

(e) Put the five numbers 799, 908, 1000, 857 and 988 in order from the greatest to the least. It is (   ).

(f) Given $\square \div \bigcirc = 3$ r 6, the least possible number for $\bigcirc$ is (   ), and in this case, then the number in $\square$ is (   ).

(g) A leap year has (   ) days, which is (   ) weeks and (   ) days.

5 Use the column method to work out these calculations. (18%)

  (a) 187＋552＝   (b) 607－268   (c) 1000－591＝

  (d) 3×278＝   (e) 124×8＝   (f) 612÷9＝

6 The diagram below consists of three squares. Answer the following questions. (6%)

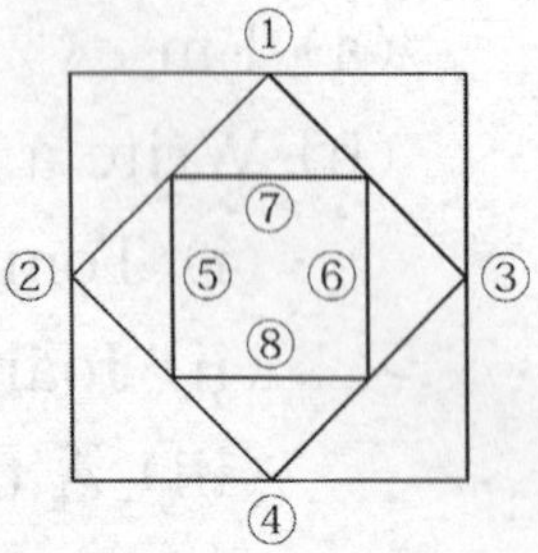

(a) How many right angles are there in total in the diagram? (　　)

(b) Write all the numbers of the vertical lines：_____

(c) Write all the numbers of the horizontal lines：_____

7 Find the perimeter of each figure. (8%)

(a) (drawing not to scale; unit：m)

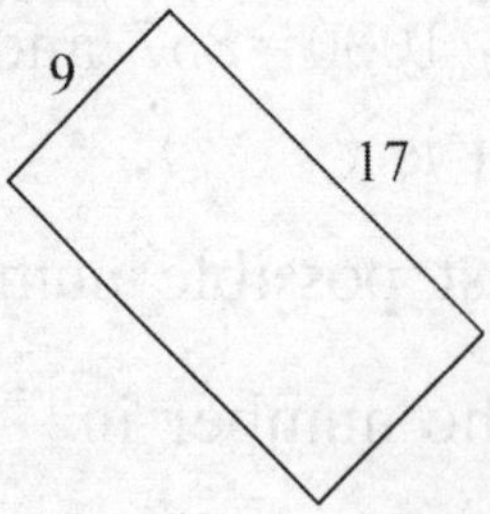

9

17

The perimeter：_____

(b) (drawing not to scale; unit：cm)

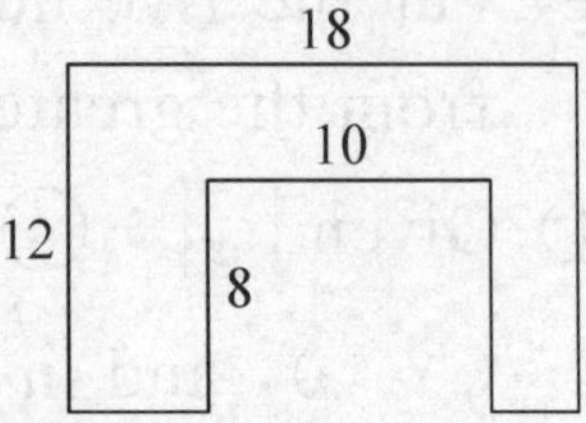

18

10

12

8

The perimeter：_____

8 Application problems. (26%. 4% each for questions (a) to (d); 10% for question (e))

(a) Tom is as tall as his father when he stands on a chair. Tom is 125 cm tall. His father is 180 cm tall. What is the height of the chair?

Number sentence：_____

(b) A box of sweets is shared by 9 children equally. Each child gets 5 sweets and there are 6 sweets left over. How many sweets were there in the box at first?

Number sentence：_____

(c) A road is 287 metres long. 8 trees will be planted in equal distance from one end of the road to the other. What is the distance between two neighboring trees?

Number sentence：_____

(d) There are 152 boys in Year 2. The number of the girls is 16 fewer than twice the number of the boys. How many girls are there in Year 2?

Number sentence：_____

(e) The table shows the number of children in Year 5 classes.

Class	Class 1	Class 2	Class 3	Class 4
Number of children	28	26	30	32

(i) Make a bar chart based on the data shown in the table above.

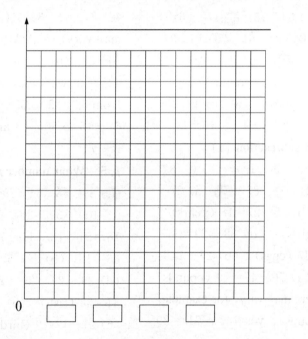

(ii) Based on the bar chart, Class (   ) has the most children and Class (   ) has the fewest children. The difference is (   ) children.

(iii) There are (   ) children in total in these four classes.

(iv) Write a question based on the bar chart and then answer it.

Question：_____

_____

Answer：_____

Answers

Chapter 1   Revising and improving

1.1   Revision for addition and subtraction of two-digit numbers

① 72 99 68 35 50 73 27 40 63 71 16 18 54 40 7 100   **②** 94 93 80 83 104 92 89 77 91   **③** 27 9 24 5 6 27 25 34 15   **④** 70 61 19 74 42 97 42 27 61   **⑤** 15 27 75 35 51 68   **⑥** (a) $18+25=43$ (pounds)   (b) $50-46=4$ (pounds)   (c) $46-18=28$ (pounds)   **⑦** (a) $1+2-3+5-4=1$ (b) $1+2+3-4+5-6=1$

1.2   Addition and subtraction (1)

① 43 55 47 55 59 100 11 0 82 51 85 46   **②** 84 57 87   **③** (a) $27+18=45$ (fruits)   (b) $45-27=18$ (pears)   (c) $25+6=31$ (girls)   (d) $38-29=9$ **④** (a) $56-19=37$ (eggs)   (b) $27+14=41$ (pages)   **⑤** (a) $76-47=29$ (pounds)   (b) 2 (toys) answers may vary, for example, $47+24=71$ (pounds), yes $100-71=29$ (pounds)

1.3   Addition and subtraction (2)

① 22 67 66 44 94 90 18 63 81 62 46 18   **②** 81 64 64 24 19 74 14 39 84 17 59 41   **③** (a) $15+10=25$ (butterflies)   (b) $38-12=26$ (chicks)   (c) $45-16=29$ (pears)   (d) $46-17=29$ (crates)   **④** (a) $32+68=100$ (pounds) a toy car and a skateboard   (b) $24+68=92$ (pounds)   (c) $54-48=6$ (pounds)   **⑤** (a) M$=7$ (b) A$=9$, M$=1$

1.4   Calculating smartly

① 2 10 6 9 5 4   **②** (a) 65   (b) 82   (c) 39   (d) 47   (e) 65   (f) 39   (g) 83 $+2$ -2 $40+43=83$ (h) 24 $+1$ $+1$ $64-40=24$ **③** (a) 12 52   (b) 59 29   (c) 16 50 66   (d) 96 50 46   (e) 46 30   (f) 29 74 44 (answer may vary)   (g) $23+70=22+71=21+72=20+73$ (h) $70-32=68-30=78-40=80-42$ (answers may vary)   **④** lines drawn from $55+28$ to $53+30$, $13+48$ to $10+51$, $62-15$ to $60-13$ and $74-36$ to $78-40$ **⑤** 74

1.5   What number should be in the box?

① 29 38 64 29 38 64 34 28 68 0 100 39 30 92 34   **②** (a) $36+18=54$ $18+36=54$ $54-18=36$ $54-36=18$ (b) 59 59 59   (c) 85 85 85   (d) 29 29 29 29 29   **③** (a) $72-34=38$ (fish)   (b) $15+36=51$ (children)   (c) $21-12=9$ (birds)   **④** $>$ $<$ $<$

1.6   Let's revise multiplication

① (a) table correctly completed   (b) multiplication facts with repeated numbers circled, for example, $2\times2=4$, $5\times5=25$ (c) multiplication facts correctly coloured   (d) The products are all multiples of 2. (answer may vary)   (e) answer may vary   **②** 8×9 to '8 times 9 is 72' to $72\div9$ $24\div8$ to '3 times 8 is 24' to 3×8 $60\div10$ to '6 times 10 is 60' to 6×10 to $60\div6$ $10\div2$ to '2 times 5 is 10' to $10\div5$ **③** answers may vary   **④** There are several ways, for example: $2\times5=1\times10$, $4\times2=2\times4=1\times8$,

$6\times3=3\times6=2\times9$, and so on.

1.7 Games of multiplication and division

1 (a) There are 3 times as many $\diamond$ as $\star$.
$9\div3=3$ (b) 5 2 10 $10\div2=5$ (c) $2\times6+5=17$ $5\times3+2=17$ $3\times6-1=17$ $6\times3-1=17$ **2** (a) $24\div6=4$ (days)
(b) $24\div3=8$ (days) (c) $24\div7=3$ (days)
r 3 **3** (a) 2 $8\div4=2$ (b) 40 $8\times5=40$ **4** 35 children

Unit test 1

1 65 9 10 2 25 97 48 4 21
89 40 7 **2** 62 6 55 76 39 72
33 31 68 **3** 17 22 79 31 40 0
10 96 4 14 2 18 **4** (a) $65-28=37$ (b) $30-16=14$ (pears) (c) $24+38=62$ (candies) (d) $45+16=61$ (storybooks)
(e) $72-37=35$ (lilies) (f) $40\div4=10$

(g) $72\div9=8$ (metres) **5**

$$\begin{array}{r} 3\ 1 \\ +\ 4\ 6 \\ \hline 7\ 7 \end{array}$$

$$\begin{array}{r} 8\ 5 \\ -\ 4\ 5 \\ \hline 4\ 0 \end{array} \qquad \begin{array}{r} 2\ 4 \\ +\ 3\ 9 \\ \hline 6\ 3 \end{array} \qquad \begin{array}{r} 6\ 6 \\ -\ 1\ 7 \\ \hline 4\ 9 \end{array}$$

Chapter 2 Multiplication and division (II)

2.1 Multiplying and dividing by 7

1 fourteen twenty-eight fifty-six
seven seven Three Seven, nine (or
vice versa) seven seventy-seven
Twelve **2** The following linked: 'Three
times seven is twenty-one' to 7×3 to $21\div7$
'Seven times eight is fifty-six' to 7×8 to
$56\div7$ 'Six times seven is forty-two' to
7×6 to $42\div6$ 'Five times seven is thirty-five' to 5×7 to $35\div5$ **3** 7 28 5 7
0 63 2 8 77 84 12 10 7 21 11
70 **4** (a) $14\div7=2$ (b) $3\times7=21$

(c) $7\times5=35$ (children) $35+6=41$
(children) **5** answers may vary, for
example, $6\times7=42$ or $14\div2=28\div4$

2.2 Multiplying and dividing by 3

1 fifteen $3\times5=15$ $5\times3=15$ $15\div3=5$
$15\div5=3$ Three eleven $3\times11=33$
$11\times3=33$ $33\div3=11$ $33\div11=3$ six
$3\times6=18$ $6\times3=18$ $18\div3=6$ $18\div6=3$
2 18 24 27 33 21 36 10 15 12
6 1 3 4 5 **3** 3 21 3 3 36
10 0 **4** (a) $3\times3=9$ (b) $15\div3=5$
(c) $3\times7=21$ **5** (a) $3\times8=24$ (pounds)
$50-24=26$ (pounds) (b) $6\times4=24$
(ducks) $24+6=30$ (ducks) **6** 6
7 younger baby monkey: $24\div(2+1)=8$
(peaches), elder baby monkey: $8\times2=16$
(peaches)

2.3 Multiplying and dividing by 6

1 $6\times3=18$ $3\times6=18$ Three times six
is eighteen. $6\times4=24$ $4\times6=24$ Four
times six is twenty-four. $6\times5=30$ $5\times6=30$ Five times six is thirty. $6\times8=48$
$8\times6=48$ Six times eight is forty-eight.
2 = > = < **3** $12=2\times6=3\times4=6\times2$ $36=4\times9=6\times6=9\times4$ $18=2\times9=3\times6=6\times3$ (answers may vary)
4 30 42 54 4 21 72 0 9 33
66 72 6 60 12 36 66 **5** $6\times8=48$ (hours) $5\times8=40$ (hours), $48-40=8$
(hours) **6** 8 **7** 25

2.4 Multiplying and dividing by 9

1 nine 9 9 twenty-seven $3\times9=27$
$9\times3=27$ thirty-six $4\times9=36$ $9\times4=36$
ninety-nine $11\times9=99$ $9\times11=99$ Six
times nine $9\times6=54$ $6\times9=54$ Two
times nine $18\div9=2$ $18\div2=9$ **2** 9
2 2 4 10 5 2 6 11 **3** $3\times7=21$
$7\times3=21$ $21\div3=7$ $21\div7=3$ $5\times9=45$ $9\times5=45$ $45\div5=9$ $45\div9=$

5 $9 \times 10 = 90$ $10 \times 9 = 90$ $90 \div 9 =$ 10 $90 \div 10 = 9$ **4** (a) $54 \div 6 = 9$ (carrots) (b) $36 \div 4 = 9$ (chocolate bars) $9 \times 3 = 27$ (bananas) $18 \div 9 = 2$ (boxes) **5** 36 20 63 127 **6** $18 \div (3-1) = 9$ (seconds) $9 \times (8-1) = 63$ (seconds)

2.5 Relationships between multiplications of 3, 6 and 9

1 $6 \times 3 = 18$ $3 \times 6 = 18$ $3 \times 6 = 18$ $6 \times 3 = 18$ $2 \times 9 = 18$ $9 \times 2 = 18$ **2** 6 3 2 9 6 12 6 9 18 **3** (a) $7 \times 6 = 42$ (b) $36 \div 4 = 9$ (c) $24 \div 3 = 8$ $24 \div 6 = 4$ **4** (a) $9 \times 2 = 18$ (tulips) $18 + 9 = 27$ (flowers) $27 \div 9 = 3$ (bouquets) (b) $6 \times 6 \div 3 = 12$ (balloons) **5** 6 **6** 36

2.6 Multiplication table

1 table correctly completed **2** twenty-eight $4 \times 7 = 28$ $7 \times 4 = 28$ $28 \div 4 = 7$ $28 \div 7 = 4$ forty $5 \times 8 = 40$ $8 \times 5 = 40$ $40 \div 5 = 8$ $40 \div 8 = 5$ sixty-six $6 \times 11 = 66$ $11 \times 6 = 66$ $66 \div 6 = 11$ $66 \div 11 = 6$ four $3 \times 4 = 12$ $4 \times 3 = 12$ $12 \div 3 = 4$ $12 \div 4 = 3$ six $4 \times 6 = 24$ $6 \times 4 = 24$ $24 \div 4 = 6$ $24 \div 6 = 4$ Four $4 \times 9 = 36$ $9 \times 4 = 36$ $36 \div 4 = 9$ $36 \div 9 = 4$ **3** (a) $10 \div 2 = 5$ Two times five is ten. 10 2 5 (b) $15 \div 3 =$ 5 Three times five is fifteen. 5 3 15 (c) $24 \div 8 = 3$ Three time eight is twenty-four. 24 8 3 (d) $9 \times 3 = 27$ Three times nine is twenty-seven. 9 3 27 **4** $2 \times 2 - 2 \times 2 = 0$ $2 \times 2 \div 2 \div 2 = 1$ $2 \div 2 + 2 \div 2 = 2$ $2 \times 2 - 2 \div 2 = 3$ (answers may vary)

2.7 Posing multiplication and division questions (1)

1 answers may vary **2** (a) 16 children took part in a relay race $16 \div 4 = 4$ (children) (b) 25 children took part in the rope skipping $25 \div 5 = 5$ (classes) (c) 42 played football.

How many children played table tennis? $42 \div 7 = 6$ (children) **3** Alex was the first runner. $100 + 20 = 120$ (metres) **4** $16 \div 2 \div 2 = 4$ (apples)

2.8 Posing multiplication and division questions (2)

1 answers may vary **2** (a) $10 \times 4 = 40$ (origami cranes) (b) $9 \times 5 = 45$ (metres) $45 + 9 = 54$ (metres) (c) $10 \times 3 = 30$ (pounds) (d) $6 \times 5 = 30$ (birds) $30 - 18 =$ 12 (birds) **3** $60 \div (3-1) = 30$ (seconds) $30 \times (6-1) = 150$ (seconds) **4** $16 \div 2 \div$ $2 = 4$ (metres)

2.9 Using multiplication and addition to express a number

1 (a) 18 $3 \times 5 + 3 = 18$ $3 \times 4 + 6 = 18$ (answers may vary) (b) 34 $4 \times 8 + 2 = 34$ $8 \times 4 + 2 = 34$ (answers may vary) **2** 7 4 5 3 5 5 4 2 7 7 10 3 5 1 9 6 4 1 6 5 9 4 11 3 **3** $32 = 3 \times 10 + 2$ $19 = 2 \times 9 + 1$ $32 = 4 \times$ $8 + 0$ $19 = 3 \times 6 + 1$ $32 = 5 \times 6 + 2$ $19 =$ $4 \times 4 + 3$ $32 = 6 \times 5 + 2$ $19 = 5 \times 3 + 4$ $32 = 7 \times 4 + 4$ $19 = 6 \times 3 + 1$ $32 = 8 \times 4 + 0$ $19 = 7 \times 2 + 5$ $32 = 9 \times 3 + 5$ $19 = 8 \times 2 + 3$ $32 = 10 \times 3 + 2$ $19 = 9 \times 2 + 1$ $32 = 11 \times 2 +$ 10 $19 = 10 \times 1 + 9$ $32 = 12 \times 2 + 8$ (answers may vary) **4** answers may vary **5** 36

2.10 Division with a remainder

1 (a) 7 1 $7 \times 3 + 1 = 22$ (b) 3 4 $3 \times 6 + 4 = 22$ **2** 6 3 $27 \div 4 = 6$ r 3 **3** 4 3 2 $14 \div 4 = 3$ r 2 **4** 5 r 2 3 r 2 7 r 3 7 r 1 5 r 7 6 r 1 5 r 6 6 r 7 9 r 2 **5** (a) $9 \div 4 = 2$ (bottles) r 1 (bottle) (b) $7 \times 6 + 5 = 47$ (peaches) (c) $50 \div 6 = 8$ r 2 **6** 43

2. 11 Calculation of division with a remainder (1)

1 20 3 6 2 20÷3＝6 r 2 **2** 7 3 45÷6＝7 r 3 **3** 5 5 8 4 8 9 4 10 8 **4** (a) √ (b) × (c) √ (d) √ (e) × (f) √ **5** (a) 31÷7＝4 (weeks) r 3 (days) (b) 50÷6＝8 (children) r 2 (sweets) (c) 49÷5＝9 (coats) r 4 (buttons) **6** (a) 26÷4＝6 (boats) r 2 (children) 6＋1＝7 (boats) (b) 26÷6＝ 4 (boats) r 2 (children) 4＋1＝5 (boats) (c) answers may vary

2. 12 Calculation of division with a remainder (2)

1 4 r 1 9 r 2 5 r 3 2 r 5 8 r 5 8 r 6 8 r 2 4 r 3 4 r 1 3 r 2 9 r 5 10 r 3 **2** 28 44 46 35 23 53 **3** (a) 2 3 15÷6＝2 r 3 (b) 52 8×6＋4＝52 (c) 4 4 24÷5＝4 r 4 (d) 1—5 5 47 (e) 7 5 5 **4** 3 1 4 1 26÷4＝6 r 2 26÷6＝4 r 2 **5** (a) 25÷6＝4 (bouquets) r 1 (flower) (b) 58÷7＝8 (bananas) r 2 (bananas) 7×9－58＝5 (bananas) **6** 3 76

2. 13 Calculation of division with a remainder (3)

1 20 8 7 54 4 7 r 2 32 48 2 38 50 79 33 71 **2** (a) 41 5 (b) 19 4 (c) 31 3 (d) 21 1 **3** (a) 19 17 (b) 35 28 **4** (a) 3×4＝12 (chicks) (b) 23÷4＝5 (hutches) r 3 (rabbits) 5＋ 1＝6 (hutches) (c) 50÷9＝5(kittens) r 5 (pounds) (d) 13÷5＝2 r 3 (red goldfish) **5** 6 5 6 9 (or 9 6) 8 4 (or 4 8) 7 8 (or 8 7) **6** 25

Unit test 2

1 49 23 66 12 40 8 4 r 2 11 4 0 7 100 77 9 1 (answer may vary)

2 4 (answer may vary) **2** 71 27 83 57 **3** (a) 45 － 29 ＝ 16 (b) 12 × 2 ＝ 24 (c) 3 × 3 × 3 ＝ 27 (d) 8 × 8＋3 ＝ 67 **4** (a) 5 × 4 ＝ 20 (balloons) 4 × 3 ＝ 12 (pens) 19＋23＝42 (baskets) (b) 50÷8＝6 (boxes) r 2 (packs) (c) 3 × 7＝21 (days) (d) 8 × 4＋4＝36 (flowers) (e) 5 × 9＝45 (cupcakes) 72－45＝27 (cupcakes) **5** (a) (i) 4 40÷10＝4 (ii) 12÷3＝4 12 4 3 12÷4＝3 12 4 3 (iii) 6 6 × 2＝12 (answers may vary) (b) (i) 5 9 10 11 (ii) 6 2 1 (answer may vary) 2 × 5 (answer may vary) (iii) 44－ 40＝4 (iv) less 3 (v) 39 (vi) 25 (c) (i) × (ii) √ (iii) × (d) (i) B (ii) C (iii) D

Chapter 3 Knowing numbers up to 1000

3. 1 Knowing numbers up to 1000 (1)

1 49 8 27 5 r 5 80 40 57 10 r 4 0 100 63 7 **2** (a) 306 three hundred and six 420 four hundred and twenty 404 four hundred and four 1000 one thousand (b) 605 six hundred and five 824 eight hundred and twenty-four **3** (a) 8 5 6 (b) ones second fourth (c) seven hundred and seven 7 7 693 (d) 403 four hundred and three **4** 400＋60＋2 1000＋0＋50＋0 700＋ 80＋8 390 808 **5** 60 **6** 8 8

3. 2 Knowing numbers up to 1000 (2)

1 56 26 165 39 12 62 29 1 48 **2** (a) 334 (b) 505 **3** six hundred and thirty-five three hundred and two 936 one thousand 400 **4** (a) 408 three 4 8 (b) 460 (c) 1000 5 (d) 299 301

(e) 47 ⑤ (b)

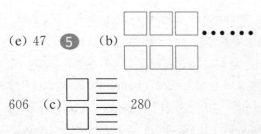

606 (c) ⬚ ☰ 280

⑥ 4 420 > 402 > 240 > 204

3.3 Number lines (in thousands) (1)

① (a) numbers correctly marked on the number line (b) A=457 B=479 C= 462 D=500 E=491 F=505

② (a) 277 279 998 1000 405 407 (b) 380 400 450 460 780 790 (c) 600 700 400 500 700 800

③ (a) 570 571 (b) 410 430 (c) 740 739 (d) 350 450 ④ (a) 439 499 (b) 888 (c) 499 501 (d) 888 > 654 > 600 > 501 > 499 > 439 > 328 > 100 > 92

⑤ (a) 499 500 501 502 503 504 (b) 100 200 300 400 500 600 700 800 (c) 100 111 122 133 144 155 166 177 188 199 ⑥ 492 663 834

⑦ 20 120 22

3.4 Number lines (in thousands) (2)

① (a) numbers correctly marked on the number line (b) 3 5 9 1 8 8 (c) 13 65 1 71 98 18 (d) b < d < a < c < e < f ② (a) 300 295 280 275 (b) 490 492 (c) 423 523 623

③ (a) 751 > 715 > 517 > 175 > 157 > 117 (b) 668 < 689 < 869 < 886 < 898 < 969 (c) 967 > 867 > 767 > 667 > 567 > 467 > 367 > 267 > 167 ④ < > > < > > < < = ⑤ 5 9 9 2 5 9 ⑥ 198−99=99 ⑦ 70÷8=8 r 6

3.5 Fun with the place value chart (1)

① 734 Seven hundred and thirty-four 430 Four hundred and thirty 301 Three

hundred and one 400 Four hundred

②

Hundreds	Tens	Ones
●●● ●●		●●●● ●●●

Hundreds	Tens	Ones
●●●● ●●●●		

③ 364 Three hundred and sixty-four

Hundreds	Tens	Ones
●●●	●●●●●●	●●●●

274 Two hundred and seventy-four

Hundreds	Tens	Ones
●●	●●●●●●●	●●●●

265 Two hundred and sixty-five

Hundreds	Tens	Ones
●●	●●●●●●	●●●●●

④ 8 ⑤ 1 1

3.6 Fun with the place value chart (2)

① 300 Three hundred

Hundreds	Tens	Ones
●●●		

210 Two hundred and ten

Hundreds	Tens	Ones
●●	●	

201 Two hundred and one

Hundreds	Tens	Ones
●●		●

120　One hundred and twenty

Hundreds	Tens	Ones
●	●●	

111　One hundred and eleven

Hundreds	Tens	Ones
●	●	●

102　One hundred and two

Hundreds	Tens	Ones
●		●●

2　153　One hundred and fifty-three

Hundreds	Tens	Ones
●	●●●●●	●●●

63　Sixty-three

Hundreds	Tens	Ones
	●●●●●●	●●●

54　Fifty-four

Hundreds	Tens	Ones
	●●●●●	●●●●

243　Two hundred and forty-three

Hundreds	Tens	Ones
●●	●●●●	●●●

144　One hundred and forty-four

Hundreds	Tens	Ones
●	●●●●	●●●●

252　Two hundred and fifty-two

Hundreds	Tens	Ones
●●	●●●●●	●●

162　One hundred and sixty-two

Hundreds	Tens	Ones
●	●●●●●●	●●

3　$600+40+3$　338　$300+0+2$　909

4　24　**5**　13

Unit test 3

1　35　40　27　9　5　32　680　31　810
79　75　70　**2**　One hundred and sixty-five 　Six hundred and eight

3　One thousand　1000　One hundred and sixty-six　166　**4**　(a) $8 \times 2 - 10 = 6$　(b) $31 - 15 + 27 = 43$　(c) $7 + 7 = 14$
5　(a) 698　702　(b) (i) numbers correctly marked on the number line
(ii) 483　500　539　578　550　(c) three hundreds　2　4　7　(d) 99　199　(e) 13
50　742　(f) 380　(g) $1000 > 968 > 806 > 405 > 380 > 45$　**6** (a)✕　(b)✓
(c)✓　(d)✓　**7** (a) C　(b) D　(c) B
(d) D　**8** $6 \times 9 = 54$ (books)　**9** $8 \times 2 + 3 \times 4 = 28$　**10**　$30 \div 4 = 7$ (cars) r 2
(children)　$7 + 1 = 8$ (cars)　**11** $34 + 18 = 52$　$52 + 28 = 80$

Chapter 4　Statistics (Ⅱ)

4.1　From statistical table to bar chart

1　(a) values correctly inserted in the table: 20 under Group A, 30 under Group B and 10 under Group C　(b) pictogram with 2 circles in Group A, 3 circles in Group B and 1 circle in group C　(c) a block diagram with shaded cells, 4 for Group A, 6 for Group B and 2 for Group C
2　values correct inserted in the table: 6 under Science, 8 under Storybook, 12

under Cartoon and 10 under Game

3 (a) 1 (b) Football swimming 5
(c) Basketball tennis (d) 35 **4** (answers
may vary)

4.2 Bar chart (1)

1 (a) 2 (b) 16 12 (c) 4 (d) 44
(e) 2 **2** (a) 16 6 10 8 20 (b) toy
airplane puppy 14 (c) 60 **3** bar
chart with correct height bars as given in
the table **4** (a) Mary Joan (b) 7
(c) 8

4.3 Bar chart (2)

1 (a) 2 11 10 (b) 23 (c) correctly
constructed and labelled bar chart
2 (a) Joan Mary John Lily Tom
(b) correctly constructed and labelled bar
chart **3** (a) 2 (b) football badminton
(c) 33 (d) 1

Unit test 4

1 1 child 5 children 2 metres 12
metres 1 unit 5 units **2** (a) 2
(b) bus 14 bicycle 6 (c) 26 (d) 42
3 (a) values correctly inserted in the
table: 7 under Brand A, 14 under Brand B,
15 under Brand C and 14 under Brand D
(b) Brand C Brand A (c) Brand B
Brand D (d) 50 **4** (a) 4 28 4
(b) bar 3 and a half units high drawn for
strawberry (c) answer may vary

Chapter 5 Introduction to time (Ⅲ)

5.1 Second and minute

1 (a) 60 (b) 60 (c) 30 (d) 600
2 times matched to correct clock faces
3 (a) seconds (b) hour (c) hours
(d) minutes **4** 30 300 45 2 100
150 1 30 1 40 **5** answers may vary
6 (a) 3:30 (b) 7:35 (c) 11:33

(d) 7:47 **7** 11:32

5.2 Times on 12-hour and 24-hour clock and in Roman numerals

1 (a) 24 (b) 12 (c) 12 (d) morning
(e) afternoon **2** 1 10 2 6 11 12
7 3 5 4 8 **3** 8:05 10:31 3:08
12:00 **4** 08:00 1:36 p.m. 11:58 p.m.
24:00 **5** 01:20 13:20 07:17 19:17
11:00 23:00 **6** 7:30 10:30, 16:30
19:30 or 4:30 p.m. 7:30 p.m. 6
7 items linked: 19:15 to 'a quarter past
seven' 22:30 to 'half past ten' 16:25 to
4:25 9:25 to 21:25

5.3 Leap years and common years

1 (a) √ (b) √ (c) × (d) √
(e) × **2** table correctly completed: 31
29 31 30 31 30 31 31 30 31
30 31 **3** (a) 30 June September
November (b) 25 December January
March May July August October
(c) February 29 (d) 366 (working may
vary) **4** (answer may vary) Years with
365 days have 28 days in February and years
with 366 days have 29 days in February.
5 (a) 28 (b) 29 (c) 365 366
(d) 2020 2024 **6** (answer may vary) for
example, twenty-ninth of February 2004
29/02/2004

5.4 Calculating the duration of time

1 > > > < > < **2** (a) 4
(b) 45 (c) 2 10 (d) 22:05 **3** (a) 8:
30 a.m. 9:00 p.m. (b) 12 30 (c) yes
40 minutes **4** 17 days **5** (a) second
promotion 10 days (b) first promotion
8 days (c) 27 days **6** 42 25

Unit test 5

1 2:23 4:41 11:52 10:09 **2** hands
correctly drawn on clock faces **3** 120
48 70 1 40 90 1 25 **4** = =

$>$ $>$ $<$ $<$ **(5)** (a) $\times$ (b) $\checkmark$ (c) $\times$ (d) $\times$ **(6)** (a) 3:38 p.m. (b) 11:40 a.m. (c) 18:30 (d) 84 **(7)** $2\times7-2=12$ (days) **(8)** 4:00 4:25 4:40 5:05 25 minutes 15 minutes 25 minutes

Chapter 6 Consolidation and enhancement

6.1 5 threes plus 3 threes equals 8 threes

(1) (a) 4 2 6 18 (b) 3 2 3 2 6 2 12 **(2)** correctly completed table: 2 times: 2 4 6 8 10 12 14 16 18 20 4 times: 4 8 12 16 20 24 28 32 36 40 6 times: 6 12 18 24 30 36 42 48 54 60 6 answer may vary, for example, $2\times5+4\times5=6\times5=30$ **(3)** 8 48 9 36 2 20 9 63 **(4)** 48 63 90 18 **(5)** 1 2 3 7 7 **(6)** $2\times9+3\times9=45$ (pounds) **(7)** 5 5 **(8)** $9\times5=8\times5+1\times5$ $9\times5=7\times5+2\times5$ $9\times5=6\times5+3\times5$ $9\times5=5\times5+4\times5$ $9\times5=3\times5+3\times5+3\times5$ (answers may vary)

6.2 5 threes minus 3 threes equals 2 threes

(1) (a) 6 3 3 6 (b) 6 3 2 3 4 3 12 **(2)** correctly completed table: 9 times: 9 18 27 36 45 54 63 72 81 90 5 times: 5 10 15 20 25 30 35 40 45 50 4 times: 4 8 12 16 20 24 28 32 36 40 4 answer may vary, for example, $9\times6-5\times6=6\times4=24$ **(3)** 3 18 1 4 3 15 3 7 21 6 5 30 **(4)** 16 42 81 18 **(5)** 2 3 10 7 7 4 **(6)** $8\times9-3\times9=45$ (pounds) **(7)** 7 8 4 5 2 2 2 3 2 **(8)** $3\times6=4\times6-1\times6$ $3\times6=5\times6-2\times6$ $3\times6=6\times6-3\times6$ $3\times6=10\times6-5\times6-2\times6$ (answers may vary)

6.3 Multiplication and division

(1) (a) 24 6 4 (b) 56 8 7 (c) 45 5 9 (d) 100 10 0 **(2)** 8 6 9 7 5 9 **(3)** (a) $42\div7=6$ (rows) (b) $42\div6=7$ (sets) (c) $6\times7=42$ (sets) **(4)** (a) $6\times6=36$ (deer) (b) $10\times4=40$ (cranes) $40>32$ the boys have made more (c) $27\div4=6$ (taxis) r 3 (people) $6+1=7$ (taxis) (d) 4 3 $31\div7=4$ r 3 **(5)** 21 cupcakes **(6)** 32

6.4 Mathematics plaza — dots and patterns

(1) Even number Even number Odd number Odd number **(2)** $8+2=10$ $6+4=10$ $6+5=11$ **(3)** (a) 11 13 15 (b) 12 14 16 (c) 20 18 16 (d) 10 13 12 15 **(4)** 5 1 3 1 **(5)** (a) answer may vary, for example, 1, 3, 5, 7, 9 (b) answer may vary, for example, 2, 4, 6, 8, 10 (c) 31 33 35 37 39 (d) 60 62 64 66 68 (e) answers may vary, for example, 20 22 24 26 **(6)** 4 9 4 16 5 5 25 9 11 6 6 36 **(7)** 9 11 13 15 10 12 14 16 10 12 14 16 odd number even number even number

6.5 Mathematics plaza — magic square

(1) The sum is 15. **(2)** $\times$ $\checkmark$ **(3)** 3 9 1 2 7 8 5 4 2 **(4)** 15: 4 9 7 8 1 6 18: 7 2 4 3 10 5 21: 6 11 5 7 9 3 **(5)** 5 7 3 5 **(6)** (answers may vary)

6.6 Numbers to 1000 and beyond

(1) 69 36 8 197 0 82 **(2)** ten thousands thousands hundreds **(3)** 3000 5000 7000 9000 11 000 **(4)** 0 9 9 9 0 1 0 0 0 8 0 2 0 0 6 **(5)** 2202 Two thousand two hundred and two 10 000 Ten thousand 5230 Five thousand two hundred and

214

thirty   4053   Four thousand and fifty-three   **6** (a) 10   100   1000   10 000
(b) ones   hundreds   ten thousands
(c) 7523   (d) 6   60   17   (e) 9999
10 000   10 001   **7** (a) 5080   5081
(b) 5656   6767   (c) 9970   9960   9950

6.7 Read, write and compare numbers to 1000 and beyond

1 80   12   51   15   85   5   50   143   38
2 6348   5050   13 004   Nine thousand and eight   Four thousand four hundred and fifteen   Nineteen thousand and six   **3** Four thousand six hundred and thirty-two $4000+600+30+2$ Two thousand five hundred and forty-seven $2000+500+40+7$ Six thousand and three $6000+0+0+3$ Two thousand and thirty $2000+0+30+0$
4 1812   4050   6500   5006   **5** > >
> > > < < < <   **6** (a) B
(b) C   (c) C   **7** (a) $209 < 367 < 627 < 736$ (b) $7800 < 8007 < 8070 < 8700$
8 (a) 95 400   (b) answers may vary, for example, 95 400   94 500   45 900
(c) answers may vary, for example, 90 045   90 054   95 004   (d) answers may vary, for example, 90 540   95 400   94 500

Unit test 6

1 24   45   4 r 4   24   63   8 r 2   100
56   6   0   25   27   36   6   **2** 6   5   4
2   **3** +   ×   ÷   ×   −   ÷   **4** =
>   <   **5** 9   72   6   36   6 (answers may vary)   56   2 (answers may vary)
6 (a) 8×8   6×7   7×8   6×8   (b) 1
8   7   2   9   4   (c) 5   25   (d) 6   35
(e) 72   (f) 3   32   5   **7** (a) 4005   6800
1052   10 039   (b) 1   5   One thousand and five   (c) $105 < 501 < 1005 < 1050 < 5001$ (d) (i) 4200   (ii) 2004   (iii) answers may vary, for example, 4020   2004

(iv) 4200   4020   2040   2400
8 (a) $6×5=30$ (cups)   (b) $32÷8=4$
(c) $27÷6=4$ (boats) r 3 (people) $4+1=5$ (boats)   (d) $2×9=18$ (pounds)
$18 > 17$ no, not enough   (e) $6×5=30$
(apples) $30 < 32$ the girls have more apples
(f) (i) correctly drawn and labelled bar chart   (answer may vary) (ii) 6   (iii) softball and gymnastics   (iv) swimming
3   badminton   (v) 48

Chapter 7   Addition and subtraction with three-digit numbers

7.1 Addition and subtraction of whole hundreds and tens (1)

1 (a) 3   2   5   (b) 4   5   9   (c) 9   3
6   (d) 6   4   2   **2** 700   600   300   600
900   500   100   400   **3** (a) 45   2   47
(b) 45   2   43   (c) 36   12   48   (d) 36
12   24   **4** 19   190   37   370   43   430
86   860   **5** =   <   =   <
6 (a) $400−230=170$ (pounds)
(b) $530+380=910$ (books)   (c) $400−380=20$ (pounds)   (d) $340+270=610$ (apple trees)   **7** □ is greater.   It is 300 greater.

7.2 Addition and subtraction of whole hundreds and tens (2)

1 170   820   200   710   880   970   220
730   500   170   230   350   **2** (a) 510
370   480   500   650   610   1000   (b) 80
150   220   290   260   190   160   **3** 800
400   330   170   630   290   1000   440
4 210   480   640   450   800   450   770
500   450   370   660   320   30   390   240
350   **5** (a) Mary: $800−200=600$(m)
Joan: $800−250=550$(m)   Mary ran faster.
(b) $250−90−110=50$ (apples)   (c) $150+280+130=560$ (stamps)

(d) $30+80+160=270$ (seats)

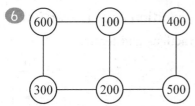

(answers may vary)

7.3 Adding and subtracting three-digit numbers and ones (1)

1 25 38 47 34 325 238 547 434
2 334 108 320 111 219 241 444
600 3 (a) 304 (b) 494 (c) 503
(d) 295 4 401 603 801 907 195
698 595 497 5 295 198 501 903
316 702 784 591 499 771 500 391
6 234 241 249 258 405 400 403
397 695 703 694 690 7 answers
may vary

7.4 Adding and subtracting three-digit numbers and ones (2)

1 333 581 717 369 272 504 297
801 698 380 262 180 2 6 5 4
1000 606 7 3 The following linked:
$627+5$ to 632 to $641-9$ $689+6$ to 695 to
$702-7$ $697+5$ to 702 to $710-8$
4 (a) $203+9=212$ (batteries) (b) $132-5=127$(cm) (c) $256-8-7=241$ (sets)
(d) $142+6-8=140$ (skips) 5 (a) $984+2=986$ or $982+4=986$ (b) $248-9=239$

7.5 Addition with three-digit numbers (1)

1 (a) 538 (b) 586 (c) 383 525
(d) 782 401 2 657 664 978 783
3 answers may vary 4 (a) $239+384=623$ (b) $574+168=742$ 5 (a) three
(b) four (c) three four

7.6 Addition with three-digit numbers (2)

1 (a) 684 (b) 434 (c) 927 (d) 515
(e) 597 (f) 785 2 (a)× 614 (b) ×

504 (c) ✓ 3 477 532 799 611
722 1000 4 $278+375=653$ $468+332=800$ $396+322=718$ 5 (a) $312+268=580$ (metres) (b) $162+135=297$
(pages) (c) $138+162=300$ (pounds)
6 781

7.7 Subtraction with three-digit numbers (1)

1 (a) 214 (b) 313 (c) 171 388
(d) 259 137 2 465 733 93 295
3 answers may vary 4 (a) $429-290=139$ (b) $695-348=347$ 5 the mass of
1 pack of salt: $630-470=160$ (grams)
the mass of 1 pack of sugar: $470-160=310$
(grams)

7.8 Subtraction with three-digit numbers (2)

1 (a) 156 (b) 41 (c) 76 (d) 168
(e) 332 (f) 29 2 (a)× 336 (b) ×
82 (c) × 66 3 604 296 181 136
178 39 4 $558-305=253$ $462-256=206$ $673-625=48$ 5 (a) $769-372=397$ (kilometres) (b) $372-112=260$
(kilometres) (c) answers may vary
6 (a) 4 (b) 3

7.9 Estimating addition and subtraction with three-digit numbers (1)

1 400 220 680 73 660 550 70
590 2 530 500 660 700 710 700
350 300 500 500 3 380 380 760
759 500 498 950 948 250 256 330
334 4 600 605 800 786 700
716 900 936 200 191 100 149
5 (a) Estimate: $230+200=430$ (children)
$430 < 450$ Yes, it is possible for Year 4
and Year 5 children to swim at the same
time (b) Estimate: $290+340=630$ (trees)
$340-290=50$ (trees) (c) (i) Estimate $80+$

110 = 190 (pounds) 190 < 200 Joan has enough money (ii) 79 + 114 = 193 (pounds) 200−193=7 (pounds)

6 (a) 264 (b) 462

7.10 Estimating addition and subtraction with three-digit numbers (2)

1 610 210 640 340 150 690 910 570 **2** 710 700 709 1000 1000 999 520 500 522 220 200 224 **3** 335 336 337 338 554 555 556 557 70 69 68 67 453 452 451 450 **4** (a) AF CE BGH (b) F E G (c) 389 591 512 630 501 404 594 538 **5** (a) (estimates may vary) $310 - 178 = 132$ (metres) (b) (estimates may vary) $244 - 156 = 88$ (metres) (c) answers may vary **6** three ways $123 + 678 = 234 + 567 = 345 + 456$ $123 + 789 = 234 + 678 = 345 + 567$ $234 + 789 = 345 + 678 = 456 + 567$

Unit test 7

1 215 162 870 220 324 295 330 218 **2** (a) 255 (b) 522 (c) 109 (d) 174 (e) 147 (f) 35 **3** (a) 400 393 600 588 200 216 200 180 (b) 510 508 390 391 110 112 360 364 **4** $402 + 148 = 550$ $662 − 266 = 396$ $800 − 482 = 318$ **5** (a) $560 − 388 = 172$ (b) $105 − 39 = 66$ (c) $288 + 109 = 397$ **6** $337 + 368 = 705$ (children) **7** $700 − 678 = 22$ (pounds) **8** $226 − 187 = 39$ (books) **9** $295 + 127 = 422$ (stamps) $422 − 250 = 172$ (stamps) **10** Cement: $215 − 36 = 179$ (tonnes) Gravel: $179 + 78 = 257$ (tonnes)

Chapter 8 Simple fractions and their addition and subtraction

8.1 Unit fractions and tenths

1 (a) $\frac{1}{2}$ (b) $\frac{1}{3}$ (c) $\frac{1}{4}$ (d) $\frac{1}{8}$ (e) $\frac{1}{10}$ (f) $\frac{4}{10}$ the unit fractions are $\frac{1}{2}$ $\frac{1}{3}$ $\frac{1}{4}$ $\frac{1}{8}$ $\frac{1}{10}$ **2** three stars circled two diamonds circled two triangles circled six triangle circled **3** (a) $\frac{2}{10}$ $\frac{4}{10}$ $\frac{5}{10}$ $\frac{6}{10}$ $\frac{7}{10}$ $\frac{8}{10}$ $\frac{9}{10}$ (b) $\frac{1}{10}$ $\frac{3}{10}$ $\frac{5}{10}$ $\frac{7}{10}$ $\frac{9}{10}$ $\frac{1}{10}$ $\frac{1}{10}$ 2 $\frac{9}{10}$ (c) $\frac{1}{10}$ $\frac{9}{10}$ 3 0 **4** (a) $\frac{1}{10}$ (b) $\frac{3}{10}$ (c) $\frac{2}{10}$ (d) $\frac{4}{10}$ (e) $\frac{1}{10}$ $\frac{2}{10}$ $\frac{3}{10}$ $\frac{4}{10}$ **5** $\frac{1}{10}$ $\frac{1}{5}$ $\frac{1}{4}$ $\frac{3}{10}$ $\frac{1}{2}$ $\frac{7}{10}$ $\frac{9}{10}$

8.2 Non-unit fractions

1 (a) $\frac{1}{9}$ $\frac{5}{9}$ $\frac{4}{9}$ (b) $\frac{1}{4}$ $\frac{3}{4}$ (c) $\frac{1}{9}$ $\frac{1}{4}$; $\frac{5}{9}$ $\frac{4}{9}$ $\frac{3}{4}$ **2** $\frac{4}{9}$ $\frac{2}{6}$ $\frac{2}{8}$ or $\frac{1}{4}$ **3** × √ √ **4** (a) $\frac{1}{7}$ $\frac{4}{7}$ (b) 2 3 6 9 **5** (a) $\frac{1}{7}$ $\frac{2}{7}$ $\frac{4}{7}$ $\frac{5}{7}$ $\frac{6}{7}$ (b) $\frac{2}{9}$ $\frac{4}{9}$ $\frac{7}{9}$ $\frac{8}{9}$ 1 **6** (a) 4 (b) 6 (c) 8 (d) 12 (e) 18 (f) 24

8.3 Equivalent fractions

1 (a) $\frac{1}{4}$ $\frac{4}{4}$ 1 (b) $\frac{6}{6}$ **2** (a) $\frac{1}{2}$ or $\frac{4}{8}$ (b) $\frac{15}{15}$ or 1 (c) $\frac{2}{3}$ or $\frac{8}{12}$ **3** (a) $\frac{10}{10}$ 1 (b) < > = (c) $\frac{4}{4}$ 1 (d) 2 (e) $\frac{4}{6}$ $\frac{1}{5}$ 1 (f) $\frac{5}{8}$ **4** lines drawn to link $\frac{1}{2}$ to $\frac{3}{6}$ $\frac{5}{6}$ to $\frac{10}{12}$ $\frac{2}{7}$ to $\frac{4}{14}$ $\frac{3}{5}$ to $\frac{6}{10}$ $\frac{4}{6}$ to $\frac{8}{12}$ $\frac{3}{4}$ to $\frac{9}{12}$ ⑤ (a) $\frac{1}{4}$

(b) $\frac{3}{9}$ or $\frac{6}{18}$ ⑥ (a) 6 8 (b) Lily

(c) no 48 is not a multiple of 5 (d) answer may vary

8.4 Addition and subtraction of simple fractions

① (a) $\frac{3}{4}$ (b) $\frac{5}{7}$ (c) $\frac{8}{8}$ 1 ② (a) $\frac{3}{5}$

(b) $\frac{4}{8}$ ③ (a) $\frac{2}{2}$ or 1 (b) $\frac{6}{7}$ (c) $\frac{4}{4}$ or 1 (d) $\frac{2}{3}$ (e) $\frac{7}{9}$ (f) $\frac{5}{5}$ or 1

④ (a) $\frac{2}{8}$ (b) $\frac{1}{2}$ (c) 0 (d) $\frac{5}{7}$ (e) $\frac{2}{4}$

(f) $\frac{4}{5}$ ⑤ (a) $\frac{3}{24}$ $\frac{4}{24}$ $\frac{5}{24}$ (b) $\frac{7}{24}$

(c) $\frac{12}{24}$ or $\frac{1}{2}$ (d) $\frac{12}{24}$ or $\frac{1}{2}$ 12 (pages)

⑥ (a) $\frac{1}{12}$ $\frac{3}{12}$ $\frac{3}{12}$ $\frac{5}{12}$ (b) $\frac{6}{12}$ $\frac{3}{12}+\frac{3}{12}=\frac{6}{12}$ (c) $\frac{3}{12}+\frac{3}{12}+\frac{5}{12}=\frac{11}{12}$ (d) Joan's

mother Joan's grandma $\frac{5}{12}-\frac{1}{12}=\frac{4}{12}$ 4

Unit test 8

① (a) $\frac{1}{10}$ $\frac{5}{10}$ 5 (b) 2 10 15

(c) $\frac{1}{6}$ four sixths $\frac{7}{8}$ (d) 4 12

(e) bigger more ② = < >

③ lines drawn to link $\frac{2}{3}$ to $\frac{4}{6}$ $\frac{4}{5}$ to $\frac{8}{10}$

$\frac{7}{8}$ to $\frac{14}{16}$ $\frac{1}{3}$ to $\frac{3}{9}$ $\frac{5}{10}$ to $\frac{4}{8}$ ④ (a) $\frac{1}{12}$

$\frac{1}{9}$ $\frac{1}{5}$ $\frac{1}{2}$ 1 (b) $\frac{2}{7}$ $\frac{4}{7}$ $\frac{5}{7}$ $\frac{6}{7}$ 1

⑤ (a) $\frac{2}{4}$ (b) $\frac{5}{9}$ (c) $\frac{10}{10}$ or 1 (d) $\frac{1}{3}$

(e) $\frac{9}{11}$ (f) $\frac{5}{5}$ or 1 (g) $\frac{4}{10}$ (h) 0 (i) $\frac{1}{8}$

⑥ (a) 14 (b) $\frac{3}{14}$ $\frac{4}{14}$ $\frac{7}{14}$ (c) $\frac{4}{14}+\frac{7}{14}=\frac{11}{14}$ (d) △ ○ $\frac{7}{14}-\frac{3}{14}=\frac{4}{14}$ ⑦ (a) $\frac{3}{12}$

(b) $\frac{6}{12}$ or $\frac{1}{2}$ (c) yes ⑧ (a) $\frac{1}{4}$ (b) $\frac{1}{8}$

(c) $\frac{1}{16}$ (d) $\frac{1}{8}$ (e) $\frac{1}{8}$ (f) (answers may vary)

Chapter 9 Multiplying and dividing by a one-digit number

9.1 Multiplying by whole tens and hundreds (1)

① 28 15 54 280 150 540 2800 1500 540 ② (a) 240 $4\times60=240$ 1000 $5\times200=1000$ (b) 3 18 180 (c) 2 ③ (a)= (b)> (c)< (d)< (e)< (f)=

④
5×70 ——— 3500
500×7 ——— 35
5×7000 ——— 350
5×7 ——— 35 000

⑤ (a) 400 (b) 2 (c) 5 (d) 4

⑥ (a) 360 (b) 1800 (c) 3208 ⑦ $500\times8=4000$ (grams), 4000 g=4 kg ⑧ $50\times8\times2\times3=2400$ (pounds)

9.2 Multiplying and dividing by whole tens and hundreds (2)

① 27 32 42 270 320 4200 2700 320 4200 2700 3200 4200 ② (a) 5 35 3500 (b) 3 ③ (a)= (b)= (c)> (d)= (e)> (f)= ④ lines drawn from 5×80 to 400, 500×8 to 4000, 50×800 to 40 000, 5×8 to 40 and 500×800 to 400 000 ⑤ (a) C (b) B

⑥ (a) $400\times4=1600$ $400+1600=2000$ (b) $300\times5=1500$ (pounds) $1500-300=1200$ (pounds) ⑦ 80 20 4000 16

160 400 32

9.3 Writing number sentences

1 (a) $6 \times 11 = 66$ (b) $30 \times 4 = 120$ (pounds)
(c) $12 \times 3 = 36$ (pounds)

2 (a) How much do 2 boxes of cashew nuts cost?
(b) How much do 2 boxes of milk cost?
(c) How many cartons of milk in 2 boxes?
(d) What is the weight of 4 sacks of rice?

4×10
2×12
2×70
2×45

3 lines drawn to match 39×8 to 312, 26×3 to 78 and 92×4 to 368 276 138×2 or 92×3 or 69×4 or 23×12 (answers may vary) **4** answers may vary **5** 8 8

9.4 Multiplying a two-digit number by a one-digit number (1)

1 $10 \times 6 = 60$ $3 \times 6 = 18$ $60 + 18 = 78$
$13 \times 6 = 78$ **2** $7 \times 74 = 518$ $26 \times 8 = 208$
$64 \times 9 = 576$ $7 \times 70 = 490$ $20 \times 8 = 160$
$60 \times 9 = 540$ $7 \times 4 = 28$ $6 \times 8 = 48$ $4 \times 9 = 36$ $490 + 28 = 518$ $160 + 48 = 208$ $540 + 36 = 576$ $2 \times 93 = 186$ $89 \times 6 = 534$ $5 \times 54 = 270$ $2 \times 90 = 180$ $80 \times 6 = 480$ $5 \times 50 = 250$ $2 \times 3 = 6$ $9 \times 6 = 54$ $5 \times 4 = 20$ $180 + 6 = 186$ $480 + 54 = 534$ $250 + 20 = 270$ **3** (a) $15 \times 8 = 120$ (children) (b) $24 \times 2 = 48$ (children) **4** $> \ < \ < \ <$

9.5 Multiplying a two-digit number by a one-digit number (2)

1 243 **2** 98 **3** 248 64 85 357

4
$$\begin{array}{r} 1\ 4 \\ \times \quad\ 4 \\ \hline 5\ 6 \end{array}$$

5
$$\begin{array}{r} 5\ 9 \\ \times \quad\ 8 \\ \hline 4\ 7\ 2 \end{array}$$

or
$$\begin{array}{r} 8\ 4 \\ \times \quad\ 8 \\ \hline 6\ 7\ 2 \end{array}$$

9.6 Multiplying a two-digit number by a one-digit number (3)

1 20 30 53 53 61 41 52 3
2 (a) 308 (b) 324 (c) 200 (d) 300
3 (a) 343 (b) 450 (c) 704
4
$$\begin{array}{r} \times \\ 9\ 9 \\ \times \quad\ 9 \\ \hline 8\ 9\ 1 \end{array}$$
$$\begin{array}{r} \times \\ 2\ 6 \\ \times \quad\ 8 \\ \hline 2\ 0\ 8 \end{array}$$
$$\begin{array}{r} \times \\ 6\ 8 \\ \times \quad\ 5 \\ \hline 3\ 4\ 0 \end{array}$$

5 lines drawn to show $25 \times 7 = 175$, $56 \times 4 = 224$, $9 \times 42 = 378$ and 5×63 and 315.
6 (a) $98 \times 4 = 392$ (pounds) (b) $57 \times 6 = 342$ (pounds) **7**
$$\begin{array}{r} 1\ 9\ 5 \\ \times \quad\ \ 8 \\ \hline 1\ 5\ 6\ 0 \end{array}$$

9.7 Multiplying a three-digit number by a one-digit number (1)

1 2400 160 6300 360 240 1600 630 2800 24 16 63 27 **2** (b) $427 = 400 + 20 + 7$ (c) $987 = 900 + 80 + 7$
(d) $634 = 600 + 30 + 4$ **3** $3 \times 316 = 948$
4 1708 3804 1850 **5** (a) 1197
(b) 837 (c) 1854 **6** $\checkmark \quad \times \quad \checkmark$
$$\begin{array}{r} 1\ 0\ 7 \\ \times \quad\quad\ 5 \\ \hline 5\ 3\ 5 \end{array}$$
7 (a) $\boxed{2}\,\boxed{9}\,\boxed{1}$ 2 5 $\boxed{0}$ 8 $\times$
$\boxed{8}$ (b) $\square = 1$ $\triangle = 7$ $\bigcirc = 2$

9.8 Multiplying a three-digit number by a one-digit number (2)

1 25 10 21 36 250 100 210 360 2500 1000 2100 3600 **2** 1440 144 **3** (a) 780 (b) 4050 (c) 2000 three four **4** 2 4 **5** (a) $120 \times 9 = 1080$ (pages) (b) $205 \times 4 = 820$ **6** B
7 1200 2400 2400 4800 (answers may vary)

9.9 Practice and exercise

1 270　91　63　4000　80　63　**2** 294　804　3360　**3** (a) $<$　(b) $>$　(c) $<$　(d) $>$　(e) $>$　(f) $=$　**4** (a) 4　(b) three　four　(c) three　200　250　**5** (a) $650 \times 7 = 4550$　(b) $4 \times 723 = 2892$　(c) $106 \times 5 = 530$　(d) $38 \times 8 = 304$　**6** $39 \times 2 = 78$ (kg)　**7** $18 \times 9 + 42 = 204$ (pages)　**8** $4 \times 26 \times 3 = 312$ (books)　**9** $708 \times 5 = 3540$　$190 \times 4 = 760$

9.10 Dividing whole tens and whole hundreds

1 (i) 2　4　8　5　20　40　80　50　(ii) 3　4　1　2　30　40　10　20　300　400　100　200　**2** 8　8　9　8　8　9　8　8　9　**3** 8　30　6　20　50　7　90　2　4　5　5　9　6　7　7　5　**4** (a) $270 \div 3 = 90$　(b) $350 \div 50 = 7$　(c) $640 \div 8 = 80$　**5** (a) $720 \div 9 = 80$ (books)　(b) $1500 \div 3 = 500$ (pounds)　(c) $240 \times 4 + 240 = 1200$ (litres)　**6** $\triangle = 3$　$\square = 20$　$\bigcirc = 9$

9.11 Dividing a two-digit number by a one-digit number (1)

1 4 r 1　6 r 1　5 r 2　6 r 2　6 r 1　7 r 1　9 r 3　9 r 2　**2** 5　6　6　6　8　8　**3** Mary: 50　10　23　4 r 3　14　14 r 3　Joan: 10　4 r 3　14 r 3　**4** 16　10　6　23　20　3　12　$70 \div 7 = 10$　$14 \div 7 = 2$　11 r 4　$70 \div 7 = 10$　$11 \div 7 = 1$ r 4　14 r 2　$60 \div 6 = 10$　$26 \div 6 = 4$ r 2　**5** (a) $95 \div 7 = 13$ r 4　(b) $75 \div 5 = 15$　(c) $5 \times 125 = 625$　**6** (a) $90 \div 6 = 15$　(b) $4 \times 25 = 100$ (toys), $100 > 96$, yes　**7** $4 + 4 - 4 - 4 = 0$　$(4 + 4) \div (4 + 4) = 1$　$4 \div 4 + 4 \div 4 = 2$　$(4 + 4) \div 4 = 3$　$(4 \times 4 + 4) \div 4 = 5$　$(4 + 4) \times 4 \div 4 = 8$

9.12 Dividing a two-digit number by a one-digit number (2)

1 3 r 2　6 r 1　7 r 7　6 r 1　8 r 3　8 r 6　5 r 3　9 r 3　**2** 39　13　23　31　12　**3** 12　32　34　25　**4** (a) $39 \div 3 = 13$　(b) $78 \div 6 = 13$　**5** (a) $(35 + 53) \div 4 = 22$ (hutches)　(b) $54 \div 2 = 27$ (children)　**6** $11 \div 4 = 2$ r 3　**7** 16 pieces

9.13 Dividing a two-digit number by a one-digit number (3)

1 6　6　7　9　5　5　**2** 5　9 r 1　4 r 2　6 r 2　5 r 2　5 r 1　3 r 4　5 r 5　**3** 5 r 2　6 r 4　7 r 2　7 r 3　18　13　16　12　**4** (a) $27 \div 3 = 9$ (children)　(b) $88 \div 5 = 17$ (bags) r 3 (balls)　(c) $78 \div 5 = 15$ (coats) r 3 (buttons)　**5** 7 erasers　or 14 erasers　or 21 erasers　or 28 erasers　or 35 erasers … (may have more answers)

9.14 Dividing a two-digit number by a one-digit number (4)

1 10　20　20　100　13　24　21　2000　**2** 32　30 r 2　16　15 r 2　**3** 20 r 3　40 r 1　10 r 5　20　10 r 6　10 r 3　10 r 5　10 r 7　**4** (a) 120　80　60　(b) 1000　600　500　**5** 400　900　2000　200　300　500　**6** (a) $82 \div 2 = 41$　(b) $900 \div 3 = 300$　(c) $640 \div 2 = 320$　(d) $320 \div 4 = 80$　**7** $210 \div 3 = 70$ (patches)　**8** in the 8th place

9.15 Dividing a two-digit number by a one-digit number (5)

1 60　360　3000　8000　23　1500　6 r 6　7000　63　210　40　400　**2** 14 r 2　30 r 1　18 r 2　12 r 1　16 r 1　10 r 4　**3** (a) $96 \div 3 = 32$　(b) $63 \div 7 = 9$ (days)　(c) $96 \div 8 = 12$ (minutes)　(d) $(39 + 45) \div 4 = 21$ (groups)　(e) $45 \div 5 = 9$, $9 < 15$, yes the remaining cans: $15 - 9 = 6$　**4** answer may vary, for example, $31 \div 7 = 4$ r 3　**5** $39 \div 7 = 5$ r 4　$71 \div 8 = 8$ r 7 (answers may vary)

Answers

9.16 Dividing a three-digit number by a one-digit number (1)

❶ 20 50 40 200 500 400 110 210
❷ 149 (books) 1 left over ❸ $637 \div 3 =$ 212 r 1 $665 \div 5 = 133$ $738 \div 6 = 123$
❹ 134 122 r 2 116 r 6 ❺ (a) $(266 - 62) \div 6 = 34$ (apples) (b) $100 \times 4 = 400$ (books) $400 \div 5 = 80$ (books) ❻ $\triangle = 9$

9.17 Dividing a three-digit number by a one-digit number (2)

❶ 20 100 30 13 300 23 92 150
❷ 6 6 10 6 8 5
❸
$$\begin{array}{r} 3\ 1 \\ 6\overline{)1\ 8\ 9} \\ \underline{1\ 8} \quad \cdots\cdots 3 \times 6 \\ 9 \\ \underline{6} \quad \cdots\cdots 1 \times 6 \\ 3 \end{array}$$

❹ 208 117 160 r 1 1409 ❺ 109 r 2 81 r 7 70 r 6 ❻ (a) $4200 \div 7 = 600$ (mosquitoes) (b) $480 \div 5 = 96$ (toy cars) $96 \div 8 = 12$ (toy cars) ❼ divided by 2 and the remainder is 0: 630, 934, 616; divided by 3 and the remainder is 1: 934, 616, 373; divided by 7 and the remainder is 5: 299
❽ Tom did it faster. Method Ⅰ: Tom's speed per hour: $304 \div 4 = 76$ (apples), Joan's speed per hour: $36 \times 2 = 72$ (apples), $76 > 72$; Method Ⅱ: Joan picked: $36 \times 2 \times 4 = 288$ (apples) in 4 hours; Tom picked: 304 apples in 4 hours. $304 > 288$

9.18 Dividing a three-digit number by a one-digit number (3)

❶ (a) 128 (b) 7254 ❷ $663 \div 7 = 94$ r 5
❸ 126 r 2 140 r 3 101 r 2 75 150 102 r 1 ❹ 38 54 2100 48 ❺ (a) √ (b) ✕ (c) ✕ (d) ✕ ❻ answers may vary, for example, Plan Ⅰ: 18 (pots) 28

(rows) $18 \times 28 = 504$ Plan Ⅱ: 24 (pots) 21 (rows) $24 \times 21 = 504$ Plan Ⅲ: 36 (pots) 14 (rows) $36 \times 14 = 504$ ❼ $80 \div 2 - 1 = 39$ (pots)

9.19 Application of division

❶ 5 r 2 4 r 5 5 r 3 3 r 2 8 r 4 7 r 5 6 r 1 8 r 2 ❷ (a) 123 3 (b) $83 \times 3 + 2 = 251$ (c) 3 (d) 1 1 0
❸ (a) $140 \div 6 = 23$ (boxes) r 2 (kg), $23 + 1 = 24$ (boxes) (b) $29 \div 7 = 4$ (boats) r 1 (child), $4 + 1 = 5$ (boats) $32 \div 7 = 4$ (boats) r 4 (children), $4 + 1 = 5$ (boats) $(29 + 32) \div 7 = 8$ (boats) r 5 (children), $8 + 1 = 9$ (boats) (c) $50 \div 8 = 6$ (pencil boxes) r 2 (pounds) (d) $147 \div 8 = 18$ (exercise books) r 3 (pieces) $8 - 3 = 5$ (pieces)
❹ $750 \div 3 = 250$ (kg) ❺ yes (Hint: When sawing a piece of wood into 2 pieces, it sawed once. Thus, when sawing the wood into 7 pieces, it sawed 6 times. $(7 - 1) \times 5 = 30$ minutes)

9.20 Finding the total price

❶ 63 16 32 80 1200 80 250 15 91 64 30 72 ❷ £42 £34 100 boxes ❸ Unit price × Quantity = Total price Total price ÷ Unit price = Quantity Total price ÷ Quantity = Unit price
❹ $105 \times 4 = 420$ (pounds) ❺ $30 \times 3 = 90$ (pounds) $24 \times 8 = 192$ (apples)
❻ (a) $660 \times 6 = 3960$ (b) $660 \div 6 = 110$ (c) $8 \times 402 + 7 = 3223$ ❼ $768 \div 8 = 96$ (boxes) ❽ $(12 - 1) \times 6 = 66$ (metres)
❾ the 16th tree

Unit test 9

❶ 240 1600 20 101 1800 5 64 3 545 50 50 300 900 90 28 15
❷ (a) 1104 (b) 130 (c) 102 r 1
❸ (a) 1228 (b) 228 (c) 275
❹ (a) $520 \div 4 = 130$ (b) $(38 \times 4) + 99 =$

251   (c) 192×7+2＝1346   (d) 69÷3＝23

⑤ (a) 300   240   300 (answers may vary)
(b) 9900   (c) 20   12   138   100   20   6
504 (answers may vary)   (d) tens   two
(e) 5   4   (f) 165   (g) 30   (h) 8   135
(i) 3   ⑥ 5200 pounds   ⑦ 634÷8＝
79 r 2   ⑧ 741÷9＝82 (books) r 3
(pieces)   9－3＝6 (pieces)   ⑨ 200－200÷
5＝160 (kg)   ⑩ (400－260)÷2＝70
(flowers)   ⑪ 35－252÷9＝7 (boxes)
⑫ 24×4＝96(kg)   96－24＝72(kg)
⑬ 9

Chapter 10   Let's practise geometry

10.1   Angles

① 4   6   1   5   ② (a)×   (b)√
(c)√   (d)√   ③ (a) C   (b) D   (c) D
④ 4   0, 4   4, 3   1, 3   0, 4   4, 3   0, 3
1, 5   0   ⑤ answer may vary   (a) must
be 90°   (b) an angle between 0° and 90°
(c) an angle between 90° and 180°
⑥ answer may vary, for example, a
vertical line from the top left vertex down
to the base   ⑦ 5

10.2   Identifying different types of lines (1)

① lines drawn to link: 'Horizontal lines'
to 'Lines that run from left to right' to the
diagram with horizontal lines   'Vertical
lines' to 'Lines that run from top to
bottom' to the diagram with vertical lines
② left diagram: vertical lines: ①   ③
horizontal lines: ②   ④   Right diagram:
vertical line: ④   horizontal   line: ①
③ correctly labelled and listed vertical
and horizontal lines   ④ (a)×   (b)×
(c)√   (d)√   ⑤ answers may vary

10.3   Identifying different types of lines (2)

① lines drawn to link: 'Perpendicular
lines' to 'Lines that meet at a right angle'
to the diagram with perpendicular lines
'Parallel lines' to 'Lines that will never
meet' to the diagram with parallel lines
② correctly labelled and listed parallel
and perpendicular lines, and 'none'
correctly shown   ③ (a) vertical   parallel
(b) horizontal   parallel   (c) perpendicular
(d) perpendicular   (e) perpendicular
④ (a)√   (b)×   (c)√   (d)×
⑤ answers may vary

10.4   Drawing 2-D shapes and making 3-D shapes

①

	Is it a 2-D or 3-D shape?	What is the name of the shape?	If it is a 2-D shape, is it a symmetrical figure?
	2-D	triangle	no
	3-D	cylinder	
	2-D	square	yes
	3-D	cuboid	
	2-D	hexagon	yes
	3-D	pyramid	

② correct drawings of any rectangle,

pentagon and octagon ③ correct drawings of the shapes as described (answers may vary) ④ a cube ⑤ a triangular prism ⑥ answers may vary

10.5 Length: metre, centimetre and millimetre

① 100　10　1000　50　150　7　130　226　3　90 ② 4　110　6　6 ③ (a) cm (b) mm (c) m (d) m (e) mm　mm ④ (a) > (b) > (c) > (d) < (e) < (f) = (g) = (h) = ⑤ (a) 300 mm< 340 cm <1000 cm < 11 m 98 cm < 12 m (b) 490 mm<4 m 90 cm<600 cm<50 m ⑥ (a) 7 m 45 mm (b) 90 cm ⑦ (a) 145 cm (b) 2 m 91 cm

10.6 Perimeters of simple 2-D shapes (1)

① answers may vary ② 14 m　16 m　20 m　24 m ③ 17 cm　17 mm　26 m ④ 900 m ⑤ 11 ways　10 cm

10.7 Perimeters of simple 2-D shapes (2)

① 20 cm　18 cm　22 cm　22 cm ② 38 cm　36 cm　40 mm　475 mm ③ 110 mm　112 mm　95 mm　107 mm ④ 64 cm ⑤ no　Shape 1 and Shape 2 share the same curve connecting A and B, and the other parts of their perimeters are equal because the figure is a rectangle ⑥ (a) 66 mm (b) 300 mm

Unit test 10

① angles ①　②　⑥　⑧　right angle ② ② (a) √ (b) √ (c) √ (d) × (e) √ (f) × (g) √ (h) × ③ (a) vertical

parallel (b) horizontal　parallel (c) perpendicular (d) perpendicular (e) perpendicular ④ 800　1000　90　5　1000　10　250　566　8　80　9 ⑤ (a) C (b) D (c) A (d) C ⑥ 6 ⑦ correct drawings of the shapes as described (answers may vary) ⑧ 20 m ⑨ 128 mm　101 mm　109 mm ⑩ 52 cm ⑪ 1620 m

End of year test

① 800　60　120　6　600　97　90　110　61　0　70　205 ② (a) $\frac{4}{5}$ (b) $\frac{1}{3}$ (c) $\frac{5}{6}$ (d) $\frac{8}{11}$ (e) 0 (f) $\frac{4}{7}$ ③ (a) C (b) D (c) B (d) D ④ (a) 100　1000 (b) (i) kg (ii) seconds (iii) pounds (iv) days (c) $\frac{1}{4}$　$\frac{1}{4}$ (d) 6　8 (e) 1000, 988, 908, 857, 799 (f) 7　27 (g) 366　52　2 ⑤ (a) 739 (b) 339 (c) 409 (d) 834 (e) 992 (f) 68 ⑥ (a) 12 (b) ②　③　⑤　⑥ (c) ①　④　⑦　⑧ ⑦ (a) 52 m (b) 76 m ⑧ (a) 180−125=55 (cm) (b) 9×5+6=51 (sweets) (c) 287÷7=41 (metres) (d) 152×2−16=288 (girls) (e) (i) correctly drawn and labelled bar chart showing the data in the table (ii) 4　2　6 (iii) 116 (iv) answer may vary